A Great R(

Joanna Gutmann

Blue Ocean Publishing

The author and the publisher have taken all reasonable care to ensure that all material in this work is original, or is in the Public Domain, or is used with the permission of the original copyright owners. However, if any person believes that material for which they own the copyright has found its way into this work without permission, they should contact the author, via the publisher, who will seek to investigate and remedy any inadvertent infringement.

A Great Report

© Joanna Gutmann 2017

The right of Joanna Gutmann to be identified as the author of this work has been asserted by her in accordance with the Copyright, Designs and Patents Act 1988.

All rights reserved. No part of this publication may be reproduced, stored in a retrieval system or transmitted in any form or by any means, electronic, mechanical, photocopying, recording, scanning, or otherwise, without prior written permission of the copyright holder.

Published by Blue Ocean Publishing

http://www.blueoceanpublishing.biz

A catalogue record for this book is available from the British Library.

ISBN 978-1-907527-34-0

First published in the United Kingdom in 2017 by Blue Ocean Publishing.

Contents

Introduction

Step 1   What do I want?

Step 2   Who will read and use it?

Step 3   What do I need from them?

Step 4   What they need to know and how to plan it

Step 5   Organise and head it

Step 6   Use the sections correctly

Step 7   Communicate through charts and graphs

Step 8   Present it professionally

Step 9   Be clear and persuasive

Step 10   Write a good summary

           Example report (persuade)

           Example report (inform)

           Model answers

Introduction

What is a report?

A report is just a means of communication. You could equally inform or persuade by presentation, conversation, letter, email, etc. Reports sometimes feel like an end in themselves. Yet no accident can be had without a report, no proposal made, no update given to a meeting without the paper to support it. Not only are you giving the information needed to make a decision, but you are providing evidence for the future that the decision was based on sound evidence.

The bottom line is that a report is a document, likely to be formal in style, written in an accepted structure and style using impersonal language.

Reports usually fall into one of two broad categories: 'tell' or 'sell'.

'Tell' reports
Many reports are written to inform, usually being the regular updates to a committee or board. They may also be a one-off, for example to describe events following a problem or accident. By definition, they do not have recommendations and will often have to fitted into

standard templated sections. Sometimes the purpose is genuinely just 'giving them the figures' with no interest in what is done with them. On other occasions, it is not the writer's role to make recommendations, but it is felt necessary to draw the readers' attention to a particular fact or position ... a 'take note' type of report.

'Sell' reports

The other type of report is the one that intends to persuade or influence the reader. There is nothing underhand in this, people who make strategic decisions often do not have the 'on the ground' knowledge and rely on those with the experience to present the facts and arguments. The information should be given objectively and without bias, but the report will end with a recommendation for the preferred outcome or actions necessary.

What is a good report?

The ability to communicate clearly in writing is an essential skill and one that is recognised by readers. Their perception of your general competence will be affected by the quality of the reports you write, so it is worth putting in some work to ensure your reports reflect well on you.

A good report is:
- concise, giving only as much information as is needed by the reader;

- clear, using language that will be understood by the reader;
- focused, avoiding irrelevant (if related) information;
- structured, so it leads and guides the reader from the initial introduction to the recommendation at the end.

Why is it difficult?

For many people, report-writing slides quietly into their workload; sometimes it is listed in a job description, often it is not. There may be corporate guidance on style and layout, but little on what to actually include and how to argue your case. As a result, writers often veer between the two extremes of staring at a screen which is blank but for the word 'Introduction' typed hopefully, or a 'brain dump' of information typed as it occurs to the reader, leaving a mass of information to be sorted and organised.

One of the biggest problems faced by writers is that the majority of reports are written for committees. By definition, these are made of people with different interests, experience and knowledge so the report has to meet the needs of each without boring or patronising the others.

Using this book

The book has been written as a workbook, intended to guide you through the report-writing process, step by step.

Introduction

Each section is explained, illustrated by one or both of two examples, given below; you then have the chance to apply the technique to your own report.

To get the maximum benefit, you should complete each stage before moving on because each step builds on the one before it. If something is difficult, spend some time researching it or talking it through with a manager or colleague so you are confident before you move on.

The example reports

Martha works for the estates department of a large hospital. She is working on two reports, a 'tell' and a 'sell':

- The 'tell' is the annual report on car parking to the Estates and Facilities Sub-Committee of the board and it will ultimately be included in the summary report from that committee to the executive board. It is the first time that the subject has been included in the annual reporting system.

- The 'sell' report is being written to support the redesign of a poorly laid out car park. It has to be approved by the finance committee and she will have to present the report to their monthly meeting. Although increased revenue will cover the cost, it will take over a year and financial pressures mean that it will be difficult to persuade the committee to approve the idea.

Throughout the book, the examples are explained in a box like those below:

Introduction

Example report (tell, to inform)

Annual report

Example report (sell, to persuade)

Car park 6

Your report

Throughout the book, after the examples, you will find space to work on report that relates to your work. These are indicated by the pen logo.

Although you can read through the book and learn from the examples, you will achieve the best outcome by working on a report from your workplace at the same time. Try to find an example which is a 'sell' – something which needs to persuade the reader because that will enable you to use it for every stage.

Alternatively, look for a 'take note' report – something which is apparently a 'tell' (just giving information) but where you want the readers to take note of something specific.

It doesn't have to be a real example but it does need to be something you understand and are comfortable with. If you have already written the report, lock it in a drawer and pretend you are starting from the beginning.

The example I will use for my report:

Research

It is assumed that you have done the research and know what you are trying to achieve, what is involved, costs, etc. If not, it is time to put the book down and get to work – don't start writing until you are completely ready to do so.

Note
For the purposes of this book, it is assumed that your report will be read by a board or committee so reference is made to 'readers' throughout.

Step 1 | What do I want?

The first thing is to get clear is what it is that you are trying to get over to your reader. Remember, you could inform or persuade by telephone call, meeting or presentation, so it's important to start by forgetting the means and focus on the content.

For SELL reports, those that persuade
This is a simple 'bottom line' statement, just a few words to define the point of all this work.

Examples:

Through this report, I want to achieve:
- the budget staying the same next year
- investment in [project]
- a year's trial of employing modern apprentices
- restructuring the HR records
- and upgrade to Office 365
- keep the catering contract with [company]

Note that these are all very casual in style. No-one else will see this, it is simply to focus your mind on what you are doing; so forget the management speak and jargon and get to the bottom line.

Step 1: What do I want?

Example report (car park 6) – **what I want**

I want to redesign car park 6 and change to pay-on-foot parking

For TELL reports, those that inform
This is a little harder when there is nothing specific you are trying to achieve. It may be that you are genuinely just throwing the information at them, in which case this section is not relevant to you. However, you might find it worth asking yourself:

> "What would I want them to say to a colleague/PA/manager on return to the office?

In other words, is there something you want to bring to their attention when it is not relevant, or not your place, to actually make recommendations?

Examples:

I would like them to comment:
- we've had a big increase in complaints this year
- we're still within budget, but only just
- there's a hell of an overspend ... with two months to go
- we're going to need to watch spending on the temporary staff

Step 1: What do I want?

Example report (annual review) – **what I want them to be aware of**

It's all OK

✏️ Take your example subject and go right back to basics: what are you trying to achieve? Look at the examples above and try to match that simplicity, informality and brevity (detail will follow very soon).

I want to achieve/them to say: ....

....

No, there's not much room... that's because you have to get it down to just a very few words!

> *Don't even think about writing a report until you are clear what it is that you want to communicate and understand whether you are writing to inform or persuade*

Step 2 | Who will read and use it?

The most important thing to remember when writing a report is that it is not about you and your knowledge; it is about the readers (and probably, their authority).

The purpose of the report is not to tell them everything you know on the subject (or to make them able to do your job – they pay you for that), it is to give them the information they need to do their job: either to approve or monitor the work you do.

Example report (car park 6) – **who will read it?**

Estates/facilities sub-committee

Example report (annual review) – **who will read it?**

Finance committee

My report will be read by:

Step 2: Who will read and use it?

It is much easier to write when it will be read by one person because you can tailor the content to that person's needs and interests. However, most reports are written for a committee or board: a group of people with different interests, priorities and concerns.

What do they know?

It is difficult to understand the readers' knowledge because it relates to the world as they 'know' it, not the truth as you know it.

For example, take the example report on car park six (a public pay-and-display, located on the adjoining site of the old community hospital):
- Abby knows it is the staff car park at the back of the site.
- Ben knows it is the small car park behind the maternity department.
- Carol knows it is hell on wheels after being stuck in a gridlock for half an hour on her way out on Friday.
- Dipak knows it is a good place to try first as there's usually a space.
- Elle knows the lanes are too narrow.

It does not matter how clearly you know what the facts are or the truth is; you will not persuade them from your start point. You have to start from their position, even if you don't like it. Remember, this is not about what you know,

Step 2: Who will read and use it?

it's about what is relevant to the reader, so get out of your shoes, walk across the floor and step into theirs!

For every report you write, find out who will be reading it and for each, think about (or research) their knowledge or involvement in the subject. You may find there's a range of knowledge, anything from complete ignorance of the subject to more expert than you. It is important to do this because it will influence the content of the report and the extent of background or explanatory information.

Many writers face the problem of this range of expertise. It leads to the need to include information for some which will bore, or be seen as patronising to, others. This is unavoidable, but there is simple way out of the problem: the use of clear and descriptive headings (see Step six for detailed guidance). These not only help the reader find what they want, they also help avoid what is irrelevant, giving a clear indication of where to start reading again.

Example report (car park 6) – **what my readers know**

Four of the five drive to work, I've checked and they all park in the staff areas (George will use board parking spaces). They've worked here for 2-5 years, user-complaints about parking won't have reached them… probably don't know much, just won't have thought about it, not really on their radar

Step 2: Who will read and use it?

Example report (annual review) – **what my readers know**

They are well-informed and familiar but it's the first time it has been a stand-alone report.

What my readers know (remember the world as <u>they</u> see it)

What do they care about?

Again, there is the problem of the varied perspectives of a group of readers, but also that their stated interests and the concerns they express don't always match their actions. For example, in the NHS you would struggle to find a board member who doesn't say that the interests of the patients come first. But watch them with a report in a board meeting and many go straight to the 'bottom line' – usually the cost.

Step 2: Who will read and use it?

Although cost is often the key concern, your readers may also be concerned about:
- patient/customer/service-user wellbeing, satisfaction
- meeting targets
- the risk of blame if it doesn't work
- improving recent negative press coverage
- impact on their personal service
- whether the decision will show them in a good light
- improving efficiency

What interests them will again impact on the choice of information to be included in the report. As with the extent of their knowledge, this is likely to vary for the different readers. If your report is going to a committee or board, the minute-taker can be an invaluable source of information and previous minutes on the subject might show what concerns were raised. You might also find guidance from a senior member of your department who attends the meetings.

Example report (car park 6) – **my readers care about**

They don't really care about car parking but will be concerned to ensure the costs will be covered by increased income. There might be some concern after recent press coverage of parking problems at the hospital

Step 2: Who will read and use it?

Example report (annual review) – **my readers care about**

It's in their remit but one of things that just 'ticks over', vaguely interested but not particularly bothered

What my readers care about/their priorities:

What authority do they have?

This is probably the easiest question to answer in this section. There is no point in asking for an allocation of the budget if your readers are not the budget holders; there's no point asking them for authority to act if they are not in a position to give that authority.

Identify what your your readers are able to do and what you are asking from them. For example, you might be looking for £5,000 to be spent on a project but your director, the reader of your report, will include this request

Step 2: Who will read and use it?

in a departmental budget request to a board committee. Therefore, your report is not asking for the £5,000, it is asking for its inclusion in the next quarterly spending plan.

Example report (car park 6) – **my readers' authority**

To allow me to do this, to allocate a budget

Example report (annual review) – **my readers' authority**

They are responsible

✏️ My readers have the authority to:

....

....

....

But what about me?

I'm the one know knows about this ... I'm the one who's got to sort it out! Having spent all this section driving the idea that it is all about the reader, it is worth clarifying your position and perspective.

Step 2: Who will read and use it?

To them, car park six is just another car park.
    To you, it's 24 fewer unhappy people who couldn't park.

To them, machines go wrong from time to time.
    To you, it's 100 calls on the help button from people who've paid but not got a ticket.

To them it's more of their pot of money spent.
    To you it's a car park problem sorted which you leave you with more time to get on with the other stuff.

And the point of this? So you make sure you minimise or leave out the information that relates to your view, because it is not relevant to your reader. For example, if reducing complaints is important to you because you have to respond to them, it will be easy to 'just mention' the benefits in terms of complaint handling from time to time. The section on reducing complaints is likely to be long and involved because it's your 'thing'. By clarifying your perspective, you can check yourself every time to write the word *complaint* to make sure that it is relevant and appropriate to the reader at that point.

> *Really work to put yourself in your readers' shoes... to see the world how they see it*

Step 3 — What do I need from them?

This section is not relevant to you if you are only 'throwing the information at them', usually the regular update reports. Although if there is anything that you particularly want them to take from the report, this section is worth considering. If you are writing to persuade, it is now time to turn the general 'want' from Step 1 into a specific request to those who can give it to you.

For a SELL report
Return to Step 1, 'What do I want?' Remind yourself what it was that you were trying to achieve.

Example report (car park 6) – **what I want**

I want to redesign car park 6 and change to pay-on-foot parking

I want:

Step 3: What do I need from them?

Now link this to the authority that you identified in Step 2, 'Who is going to read it?'

Example report (car park 6) – **my readers' authority**

To allow me to do this, to allocate a budget

They have the authority to:

Now tie the two together to define what you want from the reader. It must be precise and 'stand alone'. Ultimately it will become the recommendation and it is important that the board understand it immediately. For example, if you just recommend that they 'approve the redesign of car park 6', they might do so, but fail to allocate the budget which will make the approval meaningless. Or they might be reading back through the report looking for costs ... and give up!

Step 3: What do I need from them?

Example report (car park 6) – **specifically what I want from the readers**

I want the readers to: *allocate £64,800 for the redesign of car park six and the change to pay-on-foot parking.*

I want the readers to:

For a TELL report
Return to Step 1, 'What do I want?' and remind yourself of what it was that you wanted them to be aware of.

report (annual review) – **what I want the readers to notice**

It's all OK

Step 3: What do I need from them?

I want the readers to be aware of:

> *Imagine they interrupted you as you presented the report and asked, "What do you want from us?". What would your answer be?*

| Step 4 | What they need to know and how to plan it |

You bring knowledge; they bring power. When you are writing a report, you are not trying to tell them everything you know – they don't want to be able to do your job … and you probably don't want them to! The purpose of the report is to give them enough information to understand the issue and make the decision that is required of them.

It's easy to feel that if you tell them everything, they can pick the bits that interest them. It doesn't usually work like that, you put them off with too much, apparently irrelevant, information and you run the risk that they put the report to one side to look at when they have more time – something that's unlikely to happen.

Look back through the book and remind yourself:
- What do they know already?
- What do they care about?

Example report (car park 6) – **refocus on the reader**

They probably don't know much, not really on their radar.

They'll be concerned to ensure costs covered by increased income, maybe press comment.

Step 4: What they need to know and how to plan it

My report

Summarise what your readers know and care about:

....

....

....

....

....

Having refocused on the reader, it is time to identify the information they need to make the decision. This is the point at which many writers make a list. This is certainly better than just turning to the computer, typing a heading and starting, or staring at the blank screen waiting for inspiration, but it isn't the best way of planning a report.

The list on the following page is the items drawn up by Martha as she thought through what to include in her report on the work to car park 6.

Reading through the list, it can be seen that the order is illogical – it is written in the order in which the items occurred to the writer. It can, of course, be tidied up, but it is easy to get bogged down in cutting and pasting items, with the result that some get lost or duplications are missed.

Step 4: What they need to know and how to plan it

Lines almost worn away in car park 6
What herringbone parking is
Where car park 6 is
It's still old pay-and-display system
Brief overview of its size and design
How PoF works
Lanes very narrow in car park 6
Figures for extra money from new spaces
New signs will be needed to be sure we are legally compliant
Info on barriers, ticket/payment machines
Why herringbone should reduce accidents
Narrower lane width means can fit in extra row
Problems with pay-and-display
Reported accident figures
Notes on problem of people turning either way on entry
Costings for payment machines
Not best use of space
Herringbone parking forces one-way traffic
Cost of repainting
Benefits of extra spaces (more £ and extra parking)
Cost of removing old lines
Angled spaces are easier to get into/exit
Need road markings to guide drivers
Good opportunity to change while needs repainting
Advantages of pay-on-foot

Step 4: What they need to know and how to plan it

A better way

Cluster planning

                              Lanes narrow in car park 6
                              Reported accident figures
Lines worn away   *People turn either way*
Where car park 6 is   *Not best use of space*
Still pay/display
Overview of size/design   *>£ from extra spaces*
Opportunity to change   *Cost of barrier/mach*
                               Cost of pay machines
                  How PoF works   *Cost of repainting*
                  Prob with P&D   *Cost of removing lines*
                  Advantages PoF

What herringbone parking is
Same number of spaces but less lane   *Need barriers/ticket*
    width as one way so fit in extra row   *machines*
Herringbone parking forces one-way traffic   *2x payment machines*
Benefits to hospital and visitors
Angled spaces are easier to use   *New signs*
Reduce accidents   *Clean & repaint*
                                       Road markings

Now the content is divided into more manageable, subject-related lists, it is easier to spot duplication or items which may need to be included but not given as much weight. Individual lists will need to be tidied – for example, the largest group above could be edited to a more sensible content and order. Have a look at the cluster plan below after it was tidied up

Step 4: What they need to know and how to plan it

                        Lanes narrow in car park six
                        Not best use of space
Where car park six is   *People turn either way*
Overview of size/design *Reported accident figures*
Still pay/display
Lines worn away
Opportunity to change
                                        Cost of removing lines
                                        Cost of repainting
                                        Cost of barrier/mach
                    Prob with P&D   *Cost of pay machines*
                    How PoF works   *>£ from extra spaces*
                    Advantages PoF

       What herringbone parking is
       Same number of spaces but less lane
           width as one way so fit in extra row   *Need barriers/ticket*
       Benefits to visitors and hospital   *machines*
       Angled spaces are easier to use   *2x payment machines*
       Reduce accidents
       Herringbone parking forces one-way traffic   *Entry/exit ok*
                                                                                    Clean & repaint
                                                                                     Road markings
                                                                                     New signs

This system works well for simpler reports, but where the clusters contain a lot of information, it can take several re-writes to work out the best structure. It becomes like a lesser version of the basic list.

Step 4: What they need to know and how to plan it

PostIt® plan

This is similar to the cluster plan, but each idea is written on a different 'sticky' and taken to a wall or table where they can be arranged into groups and sub-groups. It is a flexible system because the order can be so easily changed, but can become confusing if lots of variations are tried. If you have a go at this, take a picture of each version before you make a change, in case you need to return and can't remember what was where!

Spidergram

Another way to sort out the content is using a spidergram.

Take your core idea and put it in the centre of the page. From that, draw 'legs', one for each area that will need to be covered in the report. Allocate the points you need to make to the appropriate subject.

This does not suit everyone, but it has the big advantage of easily showing main groups, sub-groups, sub-sub-groups and is, therefore, a more flexible system.

Step 4: What they need to know and how to plan it

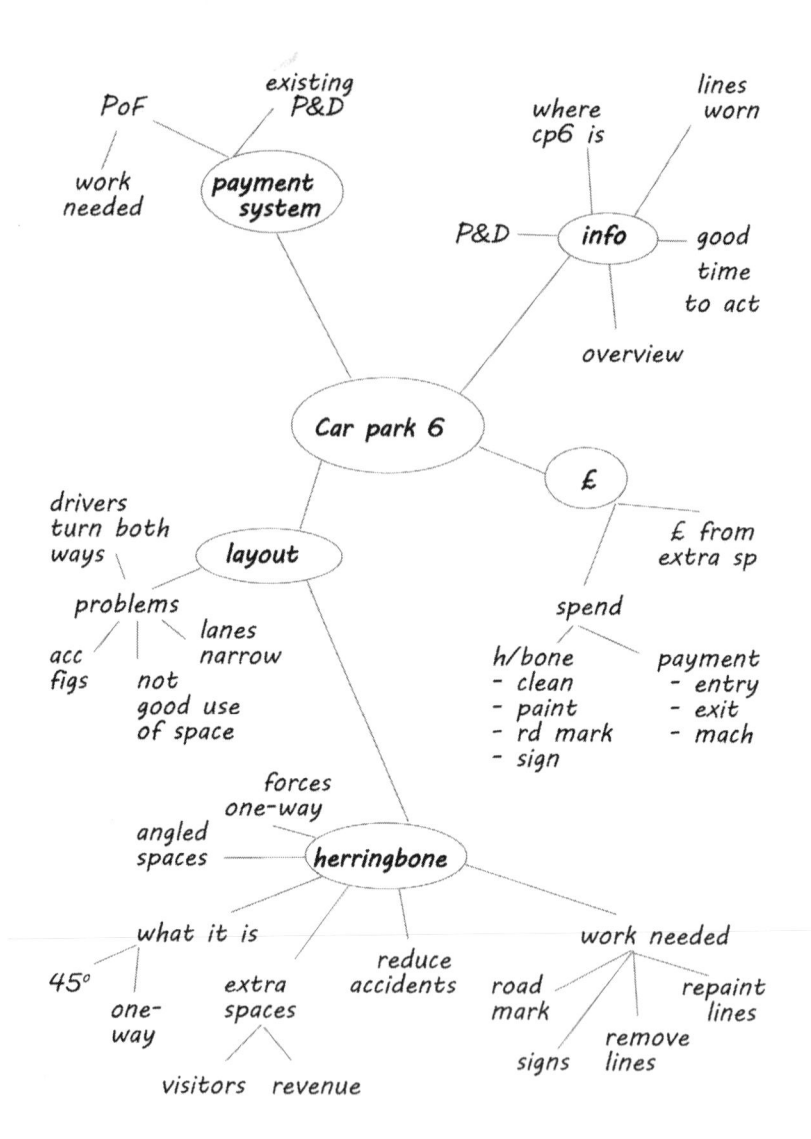

Car park 6

- **payment system**
  - PoF
    - work needed
  - existing P&D
- **info**
  - where cp6 is
  - lines worn
  - P&D
  - good time to act
  - overview
- **£**
  - £ from extra sp
  - spend
    - h/bone
      - clean
      - paint
      - rd mark
      - sign
    - payment
      - entry
      - exit
      - mach
- **layout**
  - drivers turn both ways
  - problems
    - acc figs
    - not good use of space
    - lanes narrow
- **herringbone**
  - forces one-way
  - angled spaces
  - what it is
    - 45°
    - one-way
    - extra spaces
      - visitors
      - revenue
  - reduce accidents
  - work needed
    - road mark
    - remove lines
    - signs
    - repaint lines

32

Step 4: What they need to know and ho[w]

Look at the planning methods above and
you (and the subject of your report) the

On the next page (or a separate sheet
'brain dump' – create a cluster or spi[der]
about order or priority, just focus on
groups. If you can't decide between two place[s],
item in both, but bracket it and then you can return to it
later to decide where it fits best.

> *Take as long as you need to plan, return to the plan a few times to check and review. It may well be 30% of the total time. Don't move on until you are confident that everything is relevant and sensibly grouped.*

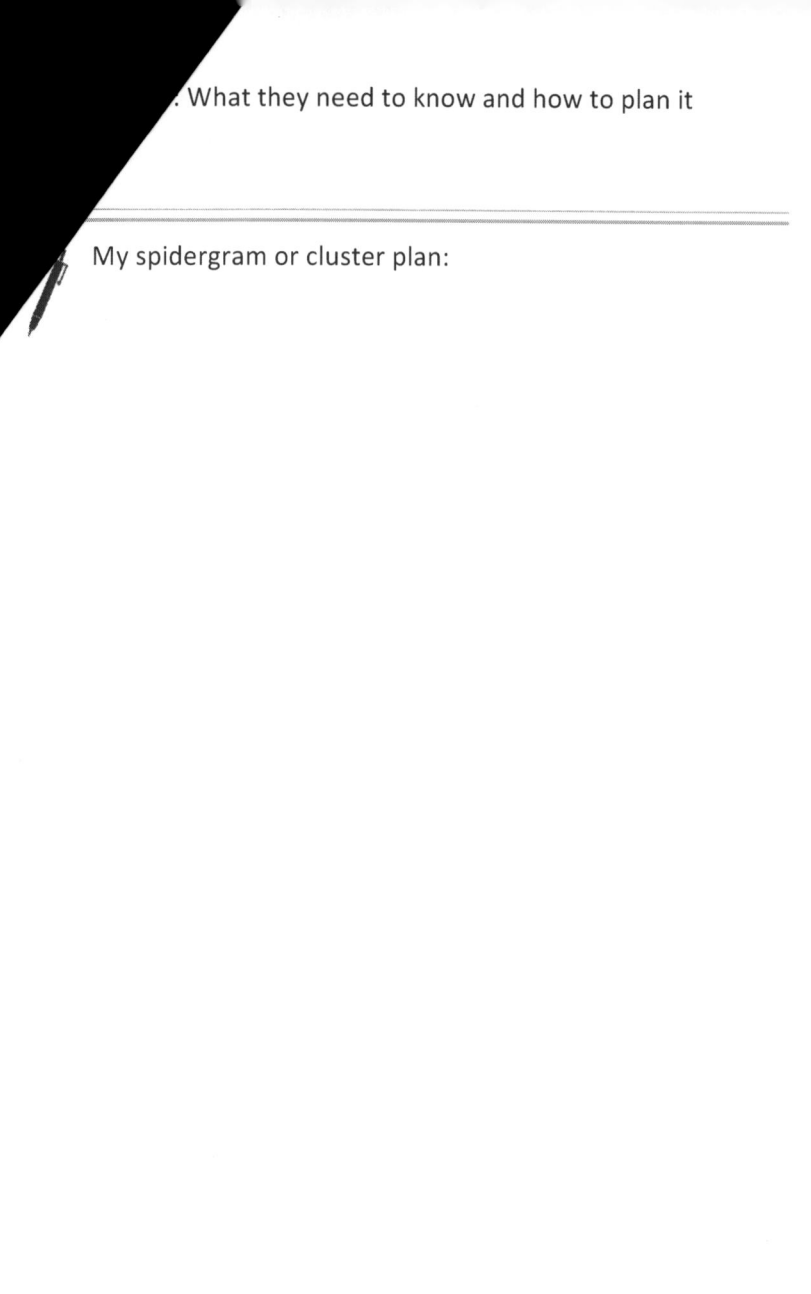

. What they need to know and how to plan it

My spidergram or cluster plan:

Step 5 Organise and head it

Look at the plan you've created, whether clusters or a spidergram, and decide on the best order for the sections.

The car park example covers four broad topics:
- Problems with parking and the herringbone layout
- Information on car park 6
- Payment for car parking
- Costs of making changes (and increased revenue)

Remember the order should be chosen to make sense to the reader. In the example above, the writer is likely to be focused on the problems (as the person who has to deal with them). The reader will come to this report with their brain still processing whatever it was they were doing before, so they need to be introduced to the subject and led through the content.

A reader-centred order would more likely be:

- Information on car park 6
- The problem and herringbone parking
- Payment for car parking
- Increased revenue and costs of making changes

Step 5: Organise and head it

✏ Transfer the topic areas from your cluster or spidergram to a list below (in any order and in words that make sense to you, we'll come to proper headings next)

✏ Now that you are looking just topics, not the content, rearrange them into an order which will be relevant to your readers

1.
2.
3.
4.
5.
6.

Reports which present alternatives

The example report relating to car park 6 that is used throughout the book is promoting one thing: the changes that the writer wants to make.

Other reports will need to present a problem or opportunity and offer different approaches so that the committee is able to choose the preferred way forward. These reports will usually still offer a recommendation but until that point the information must be given objectively. Some organisations insist on a 'do nothing' option to be explored – what will happen if no action is taken. If you have to include this, try to phrase it an alternative, not a 'do nothing' with a heading such as 'Continue with pay-and-display parking'.

Although the content of the report should guide the order of the options that are presented, the usual order is the 'continue as we are/do nothing' option first. This will be a natural progression from the information above which explains the current situation. The option that will be recommended should be given last and other options presented in the most logical order in between.

Descriptive headings

The headings you use are critically important; obviously they guide the readers to the information that individually interests them but, equally importantly, they help the reader identify and avoid the information they are not interested in.

Imagine a page of a report with nine paragraphs and no headings. The reader continues from the previous page and is interested, but on starting a new paragraph, finds this is familiar or irrelevant information, so subconsciously jumps to the next paragraph. Again, this continues to be of no interest, so again, they jump to the next paragraph. Most readers will only do this a few times before losing interest. If that irrelevant information had been headed, say 'Health and Safety Implications', the reader would have immediately been able to miss out that section and easily able to spot from the next heading where the subject changed back to something relevant to them.

Headings also break down the information into manageable chunks and help understanding, as knowledge of the topic before reading starts will increase the likelihood of the reader understanding your words at first reading.

One of the most common faults in reports is to use generic or standard headings. Look at every one and ask yourself whether it describes the content of the sections – the 'Would my grandmother understand it?' test! This applies to the main heading as well.

Choose a heading for your report, then take the core topics and give them appropriate, descriptive headings.

Step 5: Organise and head it

Example report (car park 6) – **basic skeleton**

Improvements to Car Park Six

1. **Car park six**

2. **Layout**

3. **Ticket machines**

4. **Investment & financial return**

Now look at each section of the report and see where sub-headings will be useful. At the same time bring in the standard sections of the report. In this example, information on car park 6 would be included in the introduction.

Step 5: Organise and head it

Example report (car park 6) – **full skeleton**

Improvements to Car Park Six

1. **Introduction**

2. **Layout**
    2.1 Problems with current layout
    2.2 The herringbone layout
        (a) Benefits of the herringbone layout
        (b) Reduced number of accidents
        (c) Works needed

3. **Ticket machines**
    3.1 Existing payment arrangements
    3.2 Pay-on-foot car parking
        (a) Works needed

4. **Investment and financial return**
    4.1 Investment
    4.2 Financial return

5. **Conclusion**

6. **Recommendation**

    Appendices

Step 5: Organise and head it

It is very important that you are able to see the 'skeleton' of your report – its basic structure – before you start writing. Once you start putting in the detail, you will be working with text that runs over screens or pages and it becomes harder to get, and keep hold of, the overall picture.

Having the skeleton in place is also a useful reminder of what to include. As you start including the detail, the headings should remind you what is relevant and discourage you from including irrelevant information.

Double-check each heading to ensure it is descriptive.

Step 5: Organise and head it

1. Introduction

Conclusion

Recommendation

Using a template

Many organisations now insist that reports are written into a standard template; this is usually the case for board reports. This benefits the board because the information is provided where they expect to find it; it also becomes easier to compare one report to another. However, it can be tricky for report-writers to fit the information they want to give into the standardised format.

Committee	
Date	
Report title	
Recommendation	
Summary	
Sponsors	
Author/date	
Reviewed by	
Information	
Financial implications	
Legal/compliance implications	
Link to key objective	
Equality analysis	
Privacy assessment	

It is important to be clear where the actual report is meant to be placed. Sometimes the table above is a cover sheet and the report will follow; other organisations expect the detail to be in the box named 'Information'. It is important to ensure that each box is completed correctly, as the readers will be using these to ensure that they are

Step 5: Organise and head it

discharging their decision-making duties correctly. They may also use it as quick reference point, for example, checking for the legal implications if a concern is raised during discussion in the meeting.

Almost everything discussed in the book is part of the main report section. Using the car park 6 example, the title, recommendation and summary would be moved to their boxes, the rest of the report, complete with headings, sub-headings, numbering, etc. would be in the box named 'Information'.

> *Take a final look at the skeleton as though for the first time – does it give a clear idea of the content?*

Step 6 — Use the sections correctly

As simplistic guidance, there are two types of reports: the short ones which are held together with a staple, and the long ones which will be bound. The sections may well be determined by corporate templates or guidance, the information below should be combined with whatever requirements are placed on you by your employer.

Most reports comprise an introduction, the body of the report, perhaps a conclusion, recommendation and appendices. However, there are additional sections which you may need for some reports.

Title / title page

A short report is likely to have a title typed at the top of the page together with the name of the author and the date. It will often also have the name of the organisation and/or the logo. A long report will need a cover sheet which is likely to give some or all of:

- Title
- Author (with job title and/or qualifications if appropriate)
- Who has requested the report

- Any necessary file reference number
- Confidentiality / copyright information

Summary

The summary appears first, but should be written last, when everything else is done.

The summary gives the essential 'need to know' information from the report, so that anyone who reads it in isolation gets the essential information. Although in theory it should encourage the reader to go on to read the full report, it is generally safest to work on the assumption that the summary is all they will read. As a general rule, it should be no more than one side of paper.

Summarise the report, do not report on it ("The report then details…", or "Section three describes…"). See the later section on writing the summary for a practical approach.

A **cover-sheet summary** is even smaller, usually only a paragraph or two, and is generally used where reports have a standard cover sheet. It is important to use this carefully because it will be often be copied into the minutes.

Contents page

The page lists every section with headings and sub-headings as they appear in the report, together with page numbers. Its primary use is to help readers find a section of particular interest, but it also provides a skeleton overview of the contents. It is usually only used with the long reports and is a separate sheet.

Introduction

The purpose of the introduction is to introduce the reader to the issue and to the report. It serves two purposes: to give necessary context and, less obviously, to give the more knowledgeable reader the comfort that you are both 'on the same side'.

Think of it as being like a good drinks party host who introduces you to someone with enough information to interest you and guide you towards what you might talk about.

Example report (car park 6) – **information for summary**

Car park six location, size, general layout, perhaps revenue generated

If more information or history is needed, use a **background'** section, either as a sub-section of the introduction or directly following it. Again, for the car park example, this might include more general information on parking available, the parking issues, the historical use of car park 6 (unlikely to be much relevance or use in this example!)

Step 6: Use the sections correctly

The introduction is likely to give the objective, to outline the reason for writing the report and perhaps remind the reading board members of the decision they have to make (whether to support its re-design, not that they are being asked to do so).

More lengthy and detailed reports, particularly academic ones, are also likely to need a brief description of how you approached information gathering or research and the scope/limitations of the report.

Body of the report

This is where all the necessary information should be given, It should flow smoothly from the introduction, guide the reader down a logical path to comprehension of the issue/problem and solution(s).

In many reports, there are two structures which work alongside each other: the overt and the covert. The overt structure, the 'seen' one is that which most readers recognise – introduction, report, conclusion, recommendation, which is outlined in this section. The covert structure is hidden and underpins the report, it is illustrated as the 4 Ps structure below.

The '4 Ps' structure

The '4 Ps' is a structure may not suit all reports, but is invaluable for persuasive writing:

Step 6: Use the sections correctly

Position	where we're at
Problem	why we can't stay here
Possibilities	what we can do about it
Proposal	the most effective 'solution' (recommendation)

These headings are not used in the report; it is about choosing an order for the information. The headings should be descriptive and relevant to the subject

Position
This focuses the reader's mind on the right issue. It demonstrates your understanding of the background and gives you the chance to inform those who do not know under the guise of 'let's make sure we're agreed on the start point'. Always write the position from the point of view of the reader. It can form the final part of the introduction or be separate section in its own right. The information given in the example under 'introduction' demonstrates this in use.

Problem
Although using the word problem makes it neatly fit into the mnemonic as a 'P', this section does not necessarily give bad news. Although it may be negative (sales declining, higher staff turnover or computer problems), it can be an opportunity (a new product, opportunity to cut costs, chance of a new foreign marketplace) – perhaps it could be 'potential'.

Step 6: Use the sections correctly

Example report (car park 6) – **the problem**

Car park six could fit more cars, has higher number of car park 'bumps', the lanes are very narrow

Possibilities
Sometimes a report is simply the options to act or to leave alone. In this case, this section will outline what approach you want to take. However, if you are discussing alternatives, take each in turn and explain it in detail. Give both advantages and disadvantages and be as objective as possible. Your preferred choice should not be obvious at this stage. As you present the options, the usual guidance is to finish with the one you will be recommending and start with the one which is to carry on as we are doing at the moment (or as near to it as is appropriate).

Proposal
This is the recommendation, see below.

For most business reports the main body is made of the 'problem' or 'potential' and possibilities; the position is likely to be part of the introduction and the 'proposal' is the recommendation.

Conclusion

If you report is simply promoting an option, it may not be worth including a conclusion although there is nothing wrong in doing so.

Example report (car park 6) – **information for the conclusion**

Have to do work on car park six, new design and ticketing would improve patient/visitor experience and reduce staff costs; should prove cost-neutral in around 15 months

Recommendations

This section is the fourth of the '4 Ps' and is the proposal. The recommendations should follow naturally from the main body of the report and the conclusions. They should be stated positively and should suggest, influence or urge, but try not to order.

Be clear about amounts, timescales, etc. and keep to simple terms. Again, recommendations can be made at the end of each theme, but a summary of recommendations should appear here for anyone who wants to make a quick check on them.

The recommendation(s) must stand alone. Avoid "… that the board adopt the approach outlined above". Re-state the proposed alternative clearly and simply.

Step 6: Use the sections correctly

Example report (car park 6) – **recommendation**

That the board approves the redesign of car park six and change to pay-on-foot ticketing

Alternatively

That the board allocates £64,800 for the redesign of car park six and change to pay-on-foot ticketing

For a tell report, there will be no recommendation as such because you are not asking for change. However, for board reports particularly, it is common to ask the board to 'note' the report or a particular aspect of it.

Example report (car park 6) – **recommendation**

That the board notes the 2017 car park review

This can be extended to highlight a particular issue (good news or bad!).

Example report (car park 6) – **recommendation**

That the board notes the shortage of car park spaces is causing considerable problems

Step 6: Use the sections correctly

This gives guidance for the process of the meeting by reminding the chair and minute-taker of the procedures.

Optional sections

Appendices

Appendices should contain information which is likely to interest some readers and give background or context, but which would have cluttered the main report.

For example, the report might give financial information for the current and past years, the appendix might give five years or comparison to other sites. Reading the appendices should not be essential in order to understand the report.

The appendices should be clearly numbered and should be referred to as such in the main body of the text. If you wish, you can cross reference the appendix number with the text.

References

Where you have quoted or specifically referred to any document, book, report, survey, website, etc, give full details in this section. This refers to any document, not just published works.

Bibliography / Further information

Historically, this is a list of books, websites or other published material that you used in general to compile the report. It is still used for this purpose in academic reports. In practice, for a business report, it is more commonly used to point the reader to sources of further information. It may be useful to change the heading to 'further reading' or 'information sources'.

Acknowledgements

Here you list anyone who has helped you in your research or to prepare the report. Although this is usually the first section in a book, it comes at the end of a report. It is not necessary to thank people for doing their job, but where people have gone beyond the call of duty to help you, an acknowledgement is likely to be appreciated.

Glossary

If you have to use technical terms or jargon, you can put a glossary at the end of the report. List the terms alphabetically and explain them in 'idiot's' terms. Ideally, find someone outside the organisation with no subject knowledge and find out if they understand your explanations.

Step 7 Communicate through tables, charts and graphs

Tables, charts and graphs should be used when they give the information more clearly than can be done in words. It is best to keep to the simple table, pie chart, bar/column chart or line graph. As with general layout, the defaults offered are usually not great

Location	2014	2015	2016	2017
Blue car park	£5,998	£6,134	£6,297	£6,672
Yellow car park	£3,900	£4,016	£4,157	£4,448
Long Road car park (staff)	£1,200	£1,200	£1,200	£1,200
Orange car park	£2,539	£2,694	£2,832	£3,197
Green car park	£993	£1,098	£1,234	£1,668
Car park six	£2,196	£2,454	£2,898	£3,336
Total	£16,826	£17,596	£18,618	£20,521

Note: This table, and the following ten would have a heading; they've been omitted so you can focus on the guidance and layout.

Step 7: Communicate through tables, charts and graphs

Change the column width to try to make it more equal (note that the columns for the years need to be the same size, even if one year was '10' and another was '10,000'). Align figures to the right.

Location	2014	2015	2016	2017
Blue car park	£5,998	£6,134	£6,297	£6,672
Yellow car park	£3,900	£4,016	£4,157	£4,448
Staff car park	£1,200	£1,200	£1,200	£1,200
Orange car park	£2,539	£2,694	£2,832	£3,197
Green car park	£993	£1,098	£1,234	£1,668
Car park 6	£2,196	£2,454	£2,898	£3,336
Total	£16,826	£17,596	£18,618	£20,521

Use bold for headings, totals, etc, but don't overdo it.

Location	**2014**	**2015**	**2016**	**2017**
Blue car park	£5,998	£6,134	£6,297	£6,672
Yellow car park	£3,900	£4,016	£4,157	£4,448
Staff car park	£1,200	£1,200	£1,200	£1,200
Orange car park	£2,539	£2,694	£2,832	£3,197
Green car park	£993	£1,098	£1,234	£1,668
Car park 6	£2,196	£2,454	£2,898	£3,336
Total	**£16,826**	**£17,596**	**£18,618**	**£20,521**

Step 7: Communicate through tables, charts and graphs

Change the colour of the lines from black to grey – they are meant to support the text, not dominate it.

Location	2014	2015	2016	2017
Blue car park	£5,998	£6,134	£6,297	£6,672
Yellow car park	£3,900	£4,016	£4,157	£4,448
Staff car park	1,200	£1,200	£1,200	£1,200
Orange car park	£2,539	£2,694	£2,832	£3,197
Green car park	£993	£1,098	£1,234	£1,668
Car park 6	£2,196	£2,454	£2,898	£3,336
Total	**£16,826**	**£17,596**	**£18,618**	**£20,521**

Increase the cell margins, giving a top and bottom margin of 0.05 or 0.1.

Location	2014	2015	2016	2017
Blue car park	£5,998	£6,134	£6,297	£6,672
Yellow car park	£3,900	£4,016	£4,157	£4,448
Staff car park	£1,200	£1,200	£1,200	£1,200
Orange car park	£2,539	£2,694	£2,832	£3,197
Green car park	£993	£1,098	£1,234	£1,668
Car park 6	£2,196	£2,454	£2,898	£3,336
Total	**£16,826**	**£17,596**	**£18,618**	**£20,521**

Step 7: Communicate through tables, charts and graphs

Consider whether you need vertical lines, particularly when the contents line-up neatly.

Location	2014	2015	2016	2017
Blue car park	£5,998	£6,134	£6,297	£6,672
Yellow car park	£3,900	£4,016	£4,157	£4,448
Staff car park	£1,200	£1,200	£1,200	£1,200
Orange car park	£2,539	£2,694	£2,832	£3,197
Green car park	£993	£1,098	31,234	£1,668
Car park 6	£2,196	£2,454	£2,898	£3,336
Total	**£16,826**	**£17,596**	**£18,618**	**£20,521**

Maybe you don't need all the horizontal lines either.

Location	2014	2015	2016	2017
Blue car park	£5,998	£6,134	£6,297	£6,672
Yellow car park	£3,900	£4,016	£4,157	£4,448
Staff car park	£1,200	£1,200	£1,200	£1,200
Orange car park	£2,539	£2,694	£2,832	£3,197
Green car park	£993	£1,098	31,234	£1,668
Car park 6	£2,196	£2,454	£2,898	£3,336
Total	**£16,826**	**£17,596**	**£18,618**	**£20,521**

Step 7: Communicate through tables, charts and graphs

Numbers are capital-letter-size – your table will look better with 10pt numbers instead of 12pt.

Location	2014	2015	2016	2017
Blue car park	£5,998	£6,134	£6,297	£6,672
Yellow car park	£3,900	£4,016	£4,157	£4,448
Staff car park	£1,200	£1,200	£1,200	£1,200
Orange car park	£2,539	£2,694	£2,832	£3,197
Green car park	£993	£1,098	31,234	£1,668
Car park 6	£2,196	£2,454	£2,898	£3,336
Total	**£16,826**	**£17,596**	**£18,618**	**£20,521**

If the size of the table allows it, make the table narrower than the full page – it will be more clearly a figure/table.

Location	2014	2015	2016	2017
Blue car park	£5,998	£6,134	£6,297	£6,672
Yellow car park	£3,900	£4,016	£4,157	£4,448
Staff car park	£1,200	£1,200	£1,200	£1,200
Orange car park	£2,539	£2,694	£2,832	£3,197
Green car park	£993	£1,098	31,234	£1,668
Car park 6	£2,196	£2,454	£2,898	£3,336
Total	**£16,826**	**£17,596**	**£18,618**	**£20,521**

Step 7: Communicate through tables, charts and graphs

Don't forget to give each table a title

Figure 2.4 Revenue raised from the car parks

Location	2014	2015	2016	2017
Blue car park	£5,998	£6,134	£6,297	£6,672
Yellow car park	£3,900	£4,016	£4,157	£4,448
Staff car park	£1,200	£1,200	£1,200	£1,200
Orange car park	£2,539	£2,694	£2,832	£3,197
Green car park	£993	£1,098	31,234	£1,668
Car park 6	£2,196	£2,454	£2,898	£3,336
Total	**£16,826**	**£17,596**	**£18,618**	**£20,521**

Help the 'not-numbers' people by giving the point as well.

Car park revenue has risen by a quarter in four years

Location	2014	2015	2016	2017
Blue car park	£5,998	£6,134	£6,297	£6,672
Yellow car park	£3,900	£4,016	£4,157	£4,448
Staff car park	£1,200	£1,200	£1,200	£1,200
Orange car park	£2,539	£2,694	£2,832	£3,197
Green car park	£993	£1,098	31,234	£1,668
Car park 6	£2,196	£2,454	£2,898	£3,336
Total	**£16,826**	**£17,596**	**£18,618**	**£20,521**

Figure 2.4 Revenue raised from the car parks

Step 7: Communicate through tables, charts and graphs

Pie charts

A pie chart is used to show how the whole is made up. Try to avoid more than six 'slices', and help the reader by showing the data headings around the pie chart, not as a key.

Example
Central car park continues to account for around a third of the revenue, despite not being the largest. Its proximity to the main entrance makes it the most popular choice for visitors.

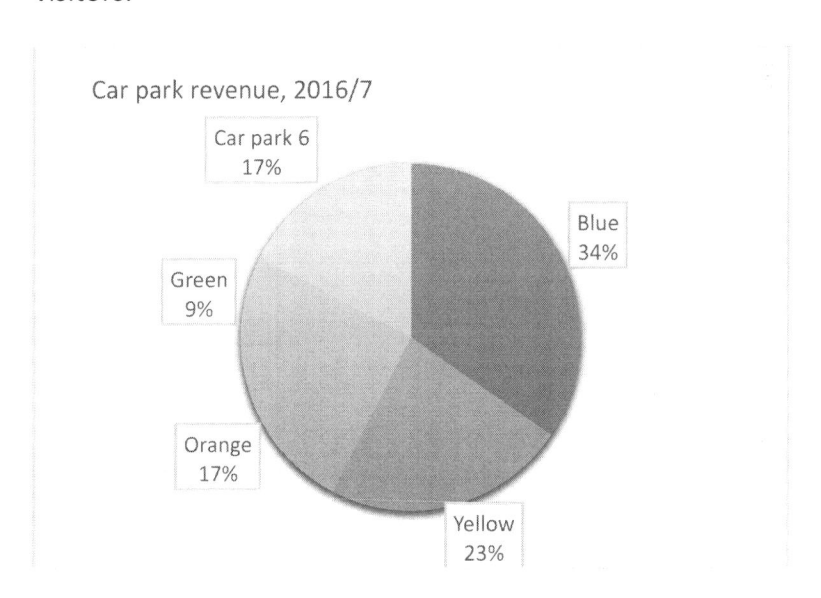

Car park revenue, 2016/7

- Car park 6: 17%
- Blue: 34%
- Green: 9%
- Orange: 17%
- Yellow: 23%

Step 7: Communicate through tables, charts and graphs

Bar charts

A bar chart is used to show comparison. They can be simple ...

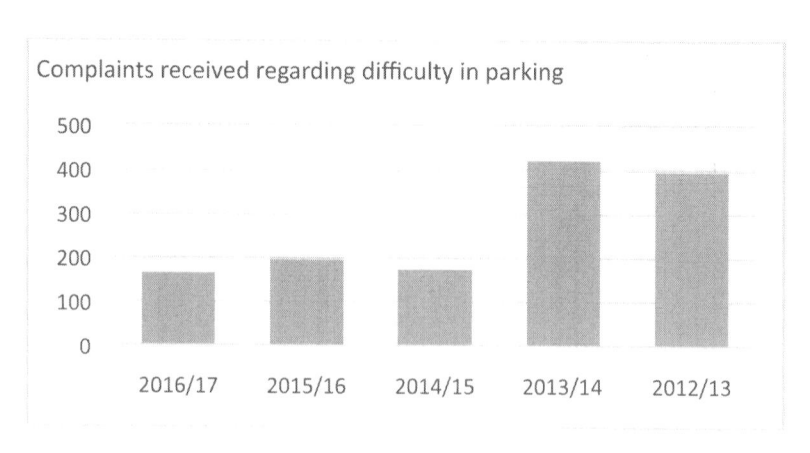

Complaints received regarding difficulty in parking

Year	Complaints
2016/17	~170
2015/16	~200
2014/15	~180
2013/14	~420
2012/13	~390

... or more complex

Cause of complaints received

Cause	2016/17	2015/16	2014/15
Difficulty in parking	~300	~290	~180
Charges	~170	~195	~175
Faulty machine	~80	~95	~100
Potholes, surface	~10	~20	~85

62

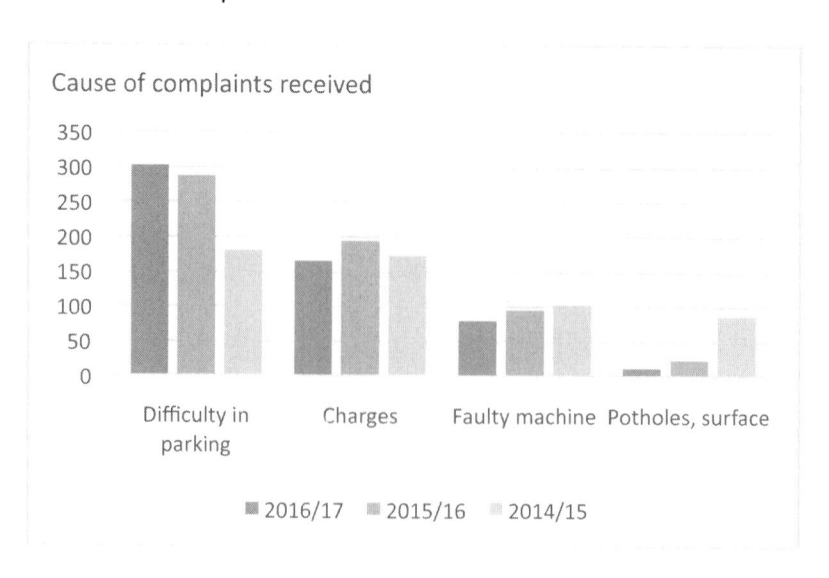

Step 7: Communicate through tables, charts and graphs

It is best to avoid 3D charts because it is difficult to read the figures accurately. In the example below, the figures are the same as in the first bar chart example. If you look at the figure for 2013/14 in the simple bar chart, it is clearly over 400. In the 3D version, it seems to be exactly 400 – this is because you should read off the side of the bar, but people generally read off the back.

Complaints received regarding difficulty in parking

If the exact figures are relevant, show them on the chart.

Complaints received regarding difficulty in parking

Year	Complaints
20012/13	165
2013/14	195
2014/15	174
2015/16	420
2016/17	395

Line chart

A line chart should be used to indicate trend.

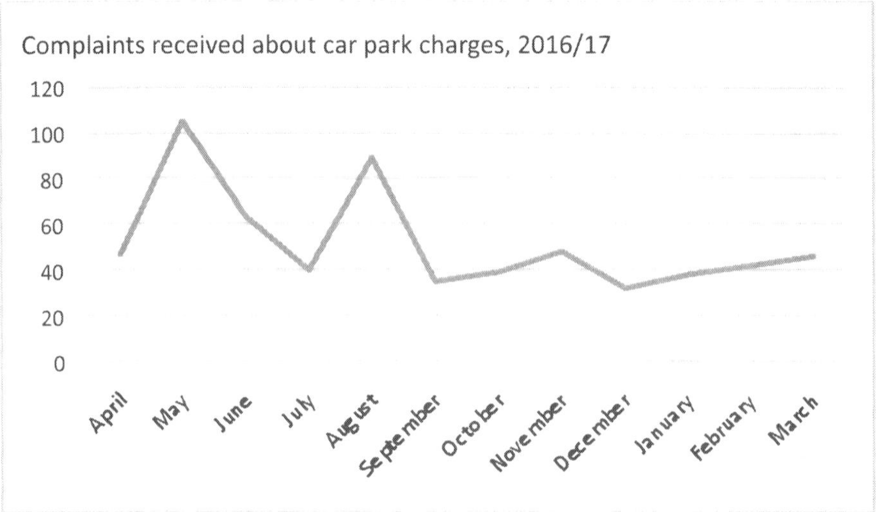
Complaints received about car park charges, 2016/17
120
100
80
60
40
20
0
April
May
June
July
August
September
October
November
December
January
February
March

Check every chart – Does it have an obvious message and a clear purpose?

Step 8 Present it professionally

Do not underestimate the importance of the visual presentation of your report. It is important on three levels:
- first impression: if it looks professional, the reader is more likely to make a sub-conscious judgement about the quality of the content;
- readability: a good layout will support the reader as they move through the document, avoiding any barriers which might be the trigger for a distracting thought of coffee or any important email;
- dyslexia: the principles of presenting a document for dyslexic readers benefit everyone.

Reports are usually presented using the defaults of the word processing program or house template. So, if you've never thought about the technicalities of presentation, here are a few simple rules.

Highlighting

Do not underline, use *italics* or type text in CAPITALS. Use the size of headings to indicate their relative importance (see the next section for guidance). Ordinary text size is usually 12 point.

Step 8: Present it professionally

6	Table layout for reports
6.1 Tables are increasingly used for reports. Often this is the result of a drive to use templates to standardise the reports that a committee has to read and understand. 6.2 The problem is that many people are not aware of how difficult these can be to read as the text is often crammed in. 6.3 The software that is commonly used to create the tables is incredibly user-<u>un</u>friendly; often acting against all the principles of readability and writing for disability. 6.4 Even if there is the requirement to use a house template, it is usually possible to make a few tweaks to make it more user-friendly	

7	A user-friendly table
7.1	Check out the cell margins). The default is usually 0.19 left and right, 0.00 top and bottom. Look at the table above; there's a small margin at the sides, nothing above and below, so the text is squashed in the cell. Change it to 0.05 or 0.01 top and bottom.
7.2	The default colour for table lines is Automatic which is black: this means that the table lines will 'fight' the text for the reader's attention. Change the line colour to grey.
7.3	Just because text is in a table, the need for paragraph spacing does not disappear. Indent, break and space paragraphs as you would outside a table.
7.4	Even where there are pre-set headings in the template, insert others based on the content of your report to guide the reader.

Ensure heading size, spacing and numbering work together

The smallest level of heading should be the same size as the text, but bold. The next level up should be a point or half a point larger, and so on. This is illustrated on the following two pages.

The guidance for spacing is:
One space between words
Two spaces between sentences
One blank line between paragraphs
Two (or 1.5) blank lines between sections

For bullet points, the space after the introductory line should be the same as the space between the bullet points. Ideally, this should be a smaller space than between paragraphs, so it is clear that the introductory line and the bullet points belong together.

Numbers should be the same size as their heading, but not bold (or the reader's eye will be drawn to the numbers before the content).

This is illustrated on the following two pages.

Step 8: Present it professionally

1. **Main heading**

   Lorem ipsum dolor sit amet, consectetur adipiscing elit. Donec ultrices et nulla nec fermentum. Pellentesque vestibulum at felis non malesuada. Fusce id lorem nisl. Nam neque tellus, ornare id convallis ac, aliquet sit amet dolor. Sed pretium odio purus, nec fringilla tortor cursus eu. Donec in arcu tristique erat malesuada tempor volutpat non eros.

   1.1 **Second-level headings**

   Praesent posuere, sapien pharetra consequat dignissim, odio urna venenatis purus, ac lacinia tellus nunc venenatis purus. In id ligula bibendum, condimentum mauris eu, iaculis diam. Nulla aliquet rutrum mauris, sollicitudin accumsan elit luctus vel.

   (a) **Third-level headings**
   Maecenas in orci convallis, convallis orci ac, elementum odio. Maecenas dapibus, dui ut tristique posuere, felis nisi rutrum orci, quis porta orci est vel arcu.

2. **Main heading**

   Duis semper porta interdum. Pellentesque tincidunt scelerisque ipsum in accumsan. Praesent vestibulum velit non dapibus interdum. Aenean aliquam tincidunt metus sit amet mollis. Aliquam a maximus tellus. Suspendisse potenti. Mauris nec maximus eros. Nam faucibus pretium tortor vitae volutpat.

3. **Main heading**

   Suspendisse potenti. Pellentesque pharetra ut nisl id cursus. Ut egestas tristique facilisis. Duis auctor neque a ultrices fermentum. Nullam finibus fermentum velit, a feugiat lectus ultricies vitae.

Step 8: Present it professionally

Or a left-aligned, blocked layout

1. **Main heading**

    Lorem ipsum dolor sit amet, consectetur adipiscing elit. Donec ultrices et nulla nec fermentum. Pellentesque vestibulum at felis non malesuada. Fusce id lorem nisl. Nam neque tellus, ornare id convallis ac, aliquet sit amet dolor. Sed pretium odio purus, nec fringilla tortor cursus eu. Donec in arcu tristique erat malesuada tempor volutpat non eros.

    1.1 **Second-level headings**

    Praesent posuere, sapien pharetra consequat dignissim, odio urna venenatis purus, ac lacinia tellus nunc venenatis purus. In id ligula bibendum, condimentum mauris eu, iaculis diam. Nulla aliquet rutrum mauris, sollicitudin accumsan elit luctus vel.

    (a) **Third-level headings**
    Maecenas in orci convallis, convallis orci ac, elementum odio. Maecenas dapibus, dui ut tristique posuere, felis nisi rutrum orci, quis porta orci est vel arcu.

2. **Main heading**

    Duis semper porta interdum. Pellentesque tincidunt scelerisque ipsum in accumsan. Praesent vestibulum velit non dapibus interdum. Aenean aliquam tincidunt metus sit amet mollis. Aliquam a maximus tellus. Suspendisse potenti. Mauris nec maximus eros. Nam faucibus pretium tortor vitae volutpat.

3. **Main heading**

    Suspendisse potenti. Pellentesque pharetra ut nisl id cursus. Ut egestas tristique facilisis. Duis auctor neque a ultrices fermentum. Etiam molestie sit amet nisi nec efficitur.

Step 8: Present it professionally

Do not justify text

Compare the two paragraphs below to those on the next page.

Justified text looks neater, but with the width of an A4 page, it can cause problems for some people with dyslexia, and will be harder to read for almost everyone. The first reason is that the size of space between the words, and even letters, will vary from one line to another, so the brain has to 'reset' itself at the start of each line. This unnatural spacing between words can make it difficult to see at a glance where a sentence ends, and larger spaces can line up vertically, making a white 'river' which divides the text unnaturally.

Have you ever been reading a magazine, read down to a picture and gone to start the next column? It can be many lines before you notice you've moved from one article to another. Your brain is behind your eyes when you are reading, so it takes a few moments before you realise something is wrong. In a document, if all the lines end in the same place, it is easy to skip or re-read a line and not realise this because you're at the end of the paragraph before you notice.

Step 8: Present it professionally

Justified text looks neater, but with the width of an A4 page, it can cause problems for some people with dyslexia, and will be harder to read for almost everyone. The first reason is that the size of space between the words, and even letters, will vary from one line to another, so the brain has to 'reset' itself as you the start of each line. This unnatural spacing between words can make it difficult to see at a glance where a sentence ends, and larger spaces can lead them to line up vertically, making a white 'river' which divides the text unnaturally.

Have you ever been reading a magazine, read down to a picture and gone to start the next column? It can be many lines before you notice you've moved from one article to another. Your brain is behind your eyes when you are reading, so it takes a few moments before you realise something is wrong. In a document, if all the lines end in the same place, it is easy to skip or re-read a line and not realise this because you're at the end of the paragraph before you notice.

Step 8: Present it professionally

Sentence and paragraph length

Compare the paragraphs below, written as too long and too short (and the good practice example on the following page.

It is too simplistic to give a simple line count as guidance for a paragraph because the length should be based on the content. However, if the paragraph gets too long, the reader is likely to subconsciously switch off part way through and move on to the next one. If you get to eight lines, it will look off-putting and the reader may struggle to keep their eye on the line. That is not to say that eight lines is a target. Generally, five or six is preferable, but if there is just one more thing to say or one more sentence, an occasional eight-line paragraph should not cause a problem. If your paragraph is growing too long, keep writing until you finish all you have to say on the subject and then read back through it. Don't just count the lines; look for places where the logic of the content determines the best place to break. If the content is familiar to the reader, the English plain and the punctuation good, the paragraphs can be a little longer. If the reader is less familiar with the content, the paragraphs will need to be shorter. It follows that if the content is familiar to the reader, the English plain and the punctuation good, the paragraphs can be a little longer. If the reader is less familiar with the content, the paragraphs will need to be shorter.

Step 8: Present it professionally

Don't lose the flow by having too short paragraphs

It is too simplistic to give a simple line count as guidance for a paragraph because the length should be based on the content.

However, if the paragraph gets too long, the reader is likely to subconsciously switch off part way through and move on to the next one.

If you get to eight lines, it will look off-putting and the reader may struggle to keep their eye on the line.

That is not to say that eight lines is a target. Generally, five or six is preferable, but if there is just one more thing to say, an occasional eight-line paragraph should not cause a problem.

If your paragraph is growing too long, keep writing until you finish all you have to say on the subject and then read back through it. Don't just count the lines; look for places where the logic of the content determines the best place to break.

If the content is familiar to the reader, the English plain and the punctuation good, the paragraph can be a little longer.

If the reader is less familiar with the content, the paragraphs will need to be shorter.

Finally, a good example

It is too simplistic to give a simple line count as guidance for a paragraph because the length should be based on the content. However, if the paragraph gets too long, the reader is likely to subconsciously switch off part way through and move on to the next one. If you get to eight lines, it will look off-putting and the reader may struggle to keep their eye on the line.

That is not to say that eight lines is a target. Generally, five or six is preferable, but if there is just one more thing to say, an occasional eight-line paragraph should not cause a problem. If your paragraph is growing too long, keep writing until you finish all you have to say on the subject and then read back through it. Don't just count the lines; look for places where the logic of the content determines the best place to break.

If the content is familiar to the reader, the English plain and the punctuation good, the paragraph can be a little longer. If the reader is less familiar with the content, the paragraphs will need to be shorter.

Step 8: Present it professionally

Two spaces after a full stop

Compare the two paragraphs below, the first with just one space after the full stop then repeated with two spaces.

There is often confusion over whether the 'two spaces after a full stop' rule is just old fashioned. In fact, it is an important aspect of readability. With modern sans serif fonts such as Arial, it is difficult to see at a glance which mark is used. Obviously the capital letter is an indicator of a new sentence, but there are so many capital letters used in business writing, many incorrectly, that they are of little help in reality.

There is often confusion over whether the 'two spaces after a full stop' rule is just old fashioned. In fact, it is an important aspect of readability. With modern sans serif fonts such as Arial, it is difficult to see at a glance which mark is used. Obviously the capital letter is an indicator of a new sentence, but there are so many capital letters used in business writing, many incorrectly, that they are of little help in reality.

Step 8: Present it professionally

Test it out

Have a look at a typed report from your workplace. At first glance, describe it in terms of it looking:
- professional
- inviting
- easy to read

Is there good 'white space' around the type?

Are the paragraphs generally under 8 lines?

Is the text left-aligned (not justified)?

Are there two spaces after a sentence?

Are there frequent, useful headings?

Is your eye is drawn to the headings, not the numbers?

Do the size and highlighting of the headings reflect their importance?

Tables, etc

Do the lines support your reading of the contents or fight for your attention?

Is the spacing of the vertical columns appropriate?

Are the charts and graphs clear with an obvious purpose and message?

Step 9 Be clear and persuasive

Write persuasively

Almost everything in this book is about persuading the reader, so a reader-centred, relevant, well-structured report which uses the most appropriate method(s) to communicate will persuade. But there are two additional techniques you might want to consider as you choose what to include:

Proof

This is what will 'prove' to your reader that your point is right. For example, you might be arguing that a rise in car park charges will not affect car park use – an idea which is not particularly well supported. There are six levels of proof which are:

1. You, the reader
2. A relation/friend
3. Someone
4. Anyone
5. Statistics
6. Darn, I'm good

You, the reader
This is the highest level of proof and it is based on subtly complimenting your reader. Imagine you work for Henrow Hospital, part of a large, multi-site trust. An example sentence would be:
> When the board approved the rise in car park charges in 2012 there was a short-term dip in revenue, but within three weeks, use had returned to the previous level and revenue for the year rose by 5%.

Look at the example report, 'Improvements to Car Park 6' at the end of the book. You'll see that section 3.2 starts with, "The main hospital site operates a pay-on-foot system …"

Using this technique, it could start with "In 2014 the board approved pay-on-foot for the main car parks, whereby …"

A relation/friend
A relation/friend can be used if your reader has not taken the same or similar action before. Consider whether a similar organisation has done it (this only works if you, the reader really identifies with the example you've chosen). An example sentence would be:
> When the board of [another hospital in the trust] approved a rise in car park charges in 2012 there was a short-term dip in revenue, but within three weeks, use had returned to the previous level and revenue for the year rose by 5%.

Step 9: Be clear and persuasive

Someone
This involves using an example which has some relevance to your reader, in this example perhaps another hospital – hopefully one they've heard of – but where there isn't the obvious link. An example would be:
> When the board of [a hospital 100 miles away] approved a rise in car park charges in 2012 there was a short-term dip in revenue, but within three weeks, use had returned to the previous level and revenue for the year rose by 5%.

Anyone
This is where the writer uses an example which may be relevant to them (a previous employer perhaps?), but has no obvious link to the reader. In this scenario, an example would be:
> When Henrow Station raised charges in 2012 there was a short-term dip in revenue, but within three weeks, use had returned to the previous level and revenue for the year rose by 5%.

Statistics
There is an assumption that statistics persuade. If that were true, no-one would smoke! Statistics provide evidence, but in themselves, they only persuade statisticians.
> NHS figures for 2014/15 show that a 5% increase in car park charges resulted in a reduction in car park usage of 3% over a period of a month, followed by a 4% rise in revenue as usage returned to normal.

Step 9: Be clear and persuasive

Darn, I'm good
At its most obvious, this includes statements such as "In my opinion," or "In the experience of the estates department". A bossy, hectoring tone also comes into this category. Whilst some people just want to be told what to do, others entrench and start coming up with arguments for the opposite point of view.

The order is not set in stone, the interests of your readers take priority, but it is useful to think where an example could be included which will just bring the reader on board; it might be a paragraph, it might be half a sentence. Once again, it's about being reader-centred.

Proof is partly about guiding you as to what to include, but it is very useful in reminding you what to leave out. In the examples above, you may have met with someone from Parkdown Hospital – it's in your home town and you had two or three meetings with them, one of which was with an old schoolfriend. Very relevant to you, but fairly meaningless to your reader and, therefore, not worth including. If you wanted to include it, you'd have to put in extra detail to show the relevance.

Features & benefits

This concept is about explaining yourself. For example, you might include a sentence which reads:
        "CCTV cameras will operate across all six car parks".

Step 9: Be clear and persuasive

You might be delighted that this is finally being put in place for personal safety reasons, but different board members see that sentence and think:

"What a waste of money."
"I won't be able to have a snooze in the car at lunchtime if they're spying on me."
"That should deter car thieves."
"People will keep asking me to view to footage to see who drove into their car."
"That will stop a few clandestine meetings."

People can read very different things into the same sentence, so be aware of the risk and add a few extra words to your report to steer the reader in the direction you want them to go:

"CCTV cameras will operate across all six car parks which will improve security for visitors and staff."

The 'take note'

With a 'tell' report, you are not seeking to persuade and give recommendations but you might want to raise the readers' awareness of a situation or problem.

This can be done overtly, perhaps by including a section clearly giving the 'potential pitfalls of X' or 'risks if Y is not implemented on time'. Alternatively, you can be more discrete with a relevant sentence here and there mentioning the pitfalls or risks.

Headings of tables and charts can be useful for the 'take note'. For example, replacing the heading "Revenue from Car Park 6" with "Revenue from Car Park 6 has continued to fall".

The ABC of plain English

A is for accurate

Be precise
Avoid vague terms such as 'as soon as possible'. Give a specific date or time instead. Similarly, do not use general words such as 'several', 'many' or 'a few' as they will mean different things to different people. Instead use specific numbers or quantities.
- ✗ *The survey will be undertaken as soon as possible*
    - ✓ *The survey will be undertaken within three months*
- ✗ *Several complaints have been received*
    - ✓ *Fourteen complaints have been received*
- ✗ *Few of the complainants mentioned making a claim*
    - ✓ *Three of the complainants mentioned making a claim*

If you are referring to documents or papers, always give enough information, so that your meaning is clear even after some time.
- ✗ *The last survey*
    - ✓ *The survey in October 2016*

Step 9: Be clear and persuasive

Give full information
If you are giving some information on a subject, make sure it is enough to make the relevance clear.
- ✗ *58% of men believe that ...*
    - ✓ *58% of men questioned in the X survey*

B is for brief

Short words
This is not about 'dumbing down', but there is no point in writing, "Users were advised that a response was required," when you could write "Users were told that an answer was needed".

Avoid Latin phrases when English words do the job.
Per se   by itself/in itself
Inter alia   among other things

Short sentences
Sentences grow too long for one of two reasons:
- a necessary full stop is replaced by 'and', 'but', 'so', and the sentence carries on.
- padding words fill out the sentence and push the word count up.

As a general rule, a sentence should be below 18 words (shorter than a couple of lines of ordinary A4). An occasional long sentence is no problem, but run the grammar checker and look for an average of 15-18 words.

Step 9: Be clear and persuasive

There is nothing wrong with a much shorter sentence, but a few of them together with lose the flow, as the reader is not sure which information belongs together.

Short paragraphs
Six lines is a good guide for maximum paragraph length. An occasional eight-liner will not be a disaster, but anything longer than that is likely to cause the reader to switch off.

Bulleted lists of long sentences / short paragraphs count as one paragraph if there is no space between the bullet points!

Again, a short paragraph presents no problem, but too many of them will disrupt the readers' understanding.

C is for clear

Use the active voice
The active voice is shorter, more direct and more easily understood than the passive voice. It is where you say 'who' before 'what'.
- ✗ *It was agreed by the board*
  - ✓ *The board agreed*
- ✗ *Installation of the signs was undertaken by the contractor*
  - ✓ *The contractor undertook the installation of the signs*

Step 9: Be clear and persuasive

Subject first
Have the subject of the sentence towards the beginning, so the reader knows what they are reading about.
- ✗ *The security team patrol the car parks daily and have noticed a significant increase in litter.*
  - ✓ *The security team have noticed a significant increase in litter during their daily patrol of the car parks.*
- ✗ *The increase in charges, particularly the three-hour rate, has led to a drop in usage in the afternoon.*
  - ✓ *Fewer cars are using the car park in the afternoon following the increase in charges, particularly the three-hour rate.*

Avoid jargon
Jargon is any term or initials which are understood by a particular group of people (and, by definition, not by those outside the group). Jargon is rife in the public sector and many find it almost impossible to express themselves without it, often because its original meaning has been lost. Remember that your report might be needed in seven years when an enquiry is being held and the readers might not be familiar with current terms.

Where jargon has to be used, use the full term and bracket the jargon afterwards and/or provide a glossary at the end of the report for those who can't find the first use of a term. Be careful though, not to bracket jargon that isn't going to be used again; just use the proper term in that case.

Step 9: Be clear and persuasive

Examples include:

Slang or current buzz words
level playing field, ring-fenced funds, deep dive,

Use of initials
DOB, DNA

Any 'in-word' or technical term within a team, department or organisation.

Word order important is
Changing the word order can change the meaning of the sentence. When checking, make sure that you have said what you meant.
I just told Angela what I had seen.
I told just Angela what I had seen.
I told Angela just what I had seen.
I told Angela what I had just seen.

Write in the positive
As in verbal communication, concentrate on the positive, telling people what they can do, or what is to happen, rather than what they can't or what isn't. Avoid double negatives.
✗   *Visitors must not walk past reception.*
    ✓ *Visitors must call at reception.*
✗   *The scheme is not suitable for those under 45 years old.*
    ✓ *The scheme is suitable for those aged 45 years or older.*
✗   *The faulty light bulbs cannot be replaced until the budgetary constraints are relaxed.*

Step 9: Be clear and persuasive

✓ *The faulty lightbulbs can be replaced when the budgetary constraints are relaxed.*

Double negatives are particularly difficult, as the reader is likely to be reading quickly and will read the positive.
✗ *This is not unreasonable.*
  ✓ *This is reasonable.*
✗ *They are not dissimilar.*
  ✓ *They are similar.*

You only need to say it once
Tautology is the pointless duplication of words – a pair of twins; it's saying the same thing twice within the phrase.
The problems were caused by frozen ice.
This is a new innovation.
Drivers return again.
Drivers circle the car park in succession, one after the other.

It happens with acronyms too.
PIN number   HIV virus
ISBN number   TSB bank

Step 9: Be clear and persuasive

Have a go, improve the following:

A is for accurate

1   The pay and display machine has recently broken down frequently.

2   Last year's quarterly report …

B is for brief

Where should the following paragraph be divided?

3   Shortage of car park spaces is an ongoing problem at the hospital which causes problems for patients and visitors, and takes staff time in handling complaints. The lines in car park 6, on the old community hospital site, are almost worn away, which results in drivers leaving excess space between cars leading to the equivalent of five spaces in each row left unused. As the lines need to be repainted, there is the opportunity to change the layout of the parking without the expenditure of a total removal of the old paint. The car park is currently 'pay-and-display' with old and increasingly unreliable ticket machines. Staff time is taken in checking tickets and emptying the machines, and attempts to tamper with the machines in order to steal the contents are increasing.

Step 9: Be clear and persuasive

Divide the following into sentences

4   Three quotes have been obtained, removing existing lines is expensive so the work required, and therefore cost, is minimised by the fact that the lines are already badly worn; the remainder of the old lines will need to be removed and the new lines painted, using thermoplastic paint for longevity, the new lines will be painted in the herringbone layout with the necessary road arrows and lines.

Find shorter, more commonly-used words to express the same point

5   Drivers are accustomed to pay-on-foot parking due to the fact that it is commonly used in public carparks

6   The charges must be seen as equitable, or drivers will attempt avoidance of payment.

C is for clear

The active voice

7   The reaction of the parking attendant ...

8   Whilst it is accepted by the security staff that the present arrangements for their overtime are unlikely to continue, should it become necessary for them to work contracted hours only, they would expect the union to support them.

Step 9: Be clear and persuasive

9. It is the belief of the board that the parking problems experienced by the hospital are the result of the decision to cancel the contract made with PayCo Machine Services in 2015.

Avoid jargon

10. A traffic light system is used to identify whether each stage in the project is completed, on target or overdue.

11. A deep dive on the figures has shown ...

Be positive

12. The arrows cannot be painted until the lines have been completed.

13. Payment cannot be made with the old £1 coin.

14. Disabled drivers will not be charged to park.

Say it once

15. There will be a forward plan to deal with potential problems and difficulties whilst the car park is closed.

16. The first priority is the safety of drivers.

17. The condition of the tarmac isn't great, but it's adequate.

Step 9: Be clear and persuasive

Problem punctuation

The punctuation marks below are those which make the writing harder to read when misused; they also cause the most concern to report writers.

Cut down the capitals

Capital letters used incorrectly, or in excess, make the writing visually harder to read and can be a barrier for readers with dyslexia. In addition, there will often be a false 'divide' – the doctor gets a capital letter, but the dinner lady does not. In fact the rules for using capital letters are generally simple.

Job titles are written with a capital when given with a name:
    Dr Alan Barker / Dr Barker
        Your doctor will advise
    Carole Durrant, Consultant Surgeon
        You will be seen by your consultant
    Toby Goodman, Production Manager
        Toby Goodman is our production manager

Proper nouns (the name) are capitalised
    Birmingham City Council
        The council
    Royal Berkshire Hospital
        The hospital

Step 9: Be clear and persuasive

    Great Western Hospitals NHS Foundation Trust
        The trust
    The Executive Board
        The board / the members
    The Estates and Facilities Committee
        The committee

Clinical conditions are only capitalised if named after someone
    Asperger's syndrome
    Parkinson's disease

You can also cut down on capitals by reducing the number of acronyms you use.

- ✘ The vehicle identification number (VIN) is a unique reference for every vehicle; the VIN can be found …

- ✓ The vehicle identification number is a unique reference for every vehicle; it can be found …

- ✓ The vehicle identification number is a unique reference for every vehicle and can be found …

- ✓ The vehicle identification number is a unique reference for every vehicle; the number can be found …

- ✘ The hospital is working with Birmingham City Council (BCC) to offer subsidised parking at the Waterside car park. BCC will make …

Step 9: Be clear and persuasive

✓ The hospital is working with Birmingham City Council to offer subsidised parking at the Waterside car park. The council will make ...

Perfect your pauses

Correct commas
There is often a comma before a quotation

> According to the conditions of use, "Vehicles must be parked within the lines of a marked parking bay".

Commas separate simple items in a list. There is no comma with the 'and' before the final item unless it's needed to make sense of the items (see the second example below).

> Pay-on-foot machines are located at the pedestrian entrance to each car park, in the main entrance hall, by the lifts on the first floor and inside the three main exits.

> Security staff can wear uniform shirts in white, pale blue, black and white, and grey. (It would, of course, be better to change the order.)

Commas can act as 'brackets', usually explaining or adding further information. They have the effect of adding two short pauses to separate this extra information from the remainder of the sentence.

> The team discussed reducing the target, currently 98%, as it was generally felt to be unrealistic.

Step 9: Be clear and persuasive

Make sure that you place the commas so that you can remove the information between them and the sentence will still make sense.

> The team discussed reducing the target as it was generally felt to be unrealistic.

The comma indicates a short pause. Only use it, when you need it.

> The comma is a simple mark, but it is often over-used, sprinkled through the sentence like confetti.

> The comma is a simple mark but it is often over-used, sprinkled through the sentence like confetti.

It may be acceptable to use a comma before 'and' if a pause improves the sentence.

> There have been many problems with the narrower parking bays, and not only from drivers of larger cars.

This will usually be when some information is 'bracketed' with commas and this falls before the 'and'.

> The car parks are checked regularly for damage, usually at the start of each month, and repairs are made on an 'as needed' basis.

Semi-colon made simple
The semi-colon is closely related to the comma, not to the colon, as its name implies. It is used when a larger/longer pause is needed.

Step 9: Be clear and persuasive

Semi-colons separate more complex items in a list. If the reader's brain has more to process, give a bigger break between items.

> The car parks which will trial the numberplate recognition are the pay-and-display public car park by the main entrance; the pay-on-foot car park by the west entrance; the main staff car park.

If any item that list includes a comma, then semi-colons must be used to separate the items.

> The car parks which will trial the numberplate recognition are the pay-and-display public car park by the main entrance; the pay-on-foot car park by the west entrance because the barriers need replacing, they regularly don't operate and people can exit without paying; the main staff car park because it was felt important to trial the system for staff as well as visitors.

Semi-colons are used in a sentence when a short pause (comma) is needed as well as a longer pause.

- ✓ Parking charges will be kept as simple as possible: a flat day rate for long-stay visitors, a top tier rate between 8.00am-4.00pm and a second tier between 4.00pm-8.00pm; there will be no charge to park between 8.00am-8.00pm
- ✓ Please obtain a letter from your consultant's office, with confirmation of the reason for the late-running of the clinic; this can be posted, faxed or emailed to us.

✗ Please obtain a letter from your consultant's office, with confirmation of the reason for the late-running of the clinic, this should be posted, faxed or emailed to us.

A semi-colon is used to indicate a pause in a sentence when it could be a full stop, but the meaning dictates that it should remain one sentence.

✓ The east car park has the new machines. North and south will get them at the end of the month.

✓ The east car park has the new machines; north and south will get them at the end of the month.

✗ The east car park has the new machines, north and south will get them at the end of the month.

In common English usage, the third of these would be unlikely to cause great offence! It is useful to know the rule because it can help if you can't decide between comma and semi-colon.

The colon
The colon is a pause with expectation; it says 'here it comes' to the reader. It is often used with 'the following', but this can be implied as well as stated.

Complaints about the car parking fell into the following three broad categories:
- The machines not working.
- The cost of parking.
- The difficulty of finding a space.

Step 9: Be clear and persuasive

Complaints about the car parking fell into three broad categories:
- The machines not working.
- The cost of parking.
- The difficulty of finding a space.

It is also used when the list is in text, rather than a displayed list, but only if a pause is needed before the first item.

Complaints about the car parking fell into three broad categories: the machines not working, the cost of parking and the difficulty of finding a space.

If no pause is needed, don't use a colon or anything else.

Complaints about the car parking fell into the three categories of the machines not working, the cost of parking and the difficulty of finding a space.

It can be used to say 'here it comes' in situations other than a list, particularly when the first part of the sentence introduces or strongly leads to the second.

Eventually the problem was identified: a Euro coin had been used in the payment machine, it had passed the first filter, but blocked the second.

Step 9: Be clear and persuasive

Test yourself, *insert commas, semi-colons or colons where needed*

1. People who use the 'help' button on the payment machines are directed to the security office however this is often not staffed.

2. The lines in the central staff car park are clearly visible those in car parks four five and six are worn but visible and don't need attention this year most lines in the West End exit car park urgently need repainting.

3. According to the Director of Estates and Facilities "Car parks have been identified as a priority for 2018/19."

4. Eventually he admitted why he hadn't reported the damage to his vehicle he had caused it himself reversing into a bollard.

5. Eventually he admitted why he hadn't reported the damage to his vehicle the accident form was completed and the file closed.

6. Numberplate recognition cameras will be installed in
   - central car park
   - car park four
   - car park six

7. Numberplate recognition cameras will be installed in central car park car park four and car park six.

8. Numberplate recognition cameras sites central car park car park four and car park six.

9. I enclose your 2017/18 parking permit please stick this on your windscreen ideally in the top left corner.

Step 9: Be clear and persuasive

10 There are nine hundred spaces in car park four six of which are for disabled users and a further 600 in car park five.

Answers are at the back of the book

Punctuating with bullet points

If the introductory line is written in such a way that it does not flow into each bullet, each should have a capital letter and full stop. If the bullet points have to be complete sentences, for example, if they are individual questions, the introductory line should be written so that it does not flow into the first bullet point.

Three car parks will trial the switch to numberplate recognition:
- The pay-and-display public car park by the main entrance, where the cameras can easily be mounted on the existing gantries.
- The pay-on-foot car park by the west entrance.
- The main staff car park.

If the introductory line flows into each bullet, and if the bullet points are short enough to need no pausing punctuation, then no punctuation is used after the initial colon.

The three car parks which will trial the numberplate recognition are the:
- pay-and-display public car park by the main entrance
- pay-on-foot car park by the west entrance
- main staff car park

Step 9: Be clear and persuasive

When the bulleted items get longer, particularly if they need other punctuation, use lower-case letters for each item, a semi-colon at the end of each and a final full stop.

> The three car parks which will trial the numberplate recognition are the:
> - pay-and-display public car park by the main entrance;
> - pay-on-foot car park by the west entrance because the barriers need replacing, they regularly don't operate and people can exit without paying;
> - main staff car park because it was felt import to trial the system for staff as well as visitors.

Hate the apostrophe?

The apostrophe is a 'hook', it warns the reader that something is going to hang on it. Although you may not know what is to hang there, just seeing the hook tells you its purpose.

> The hospital takes great care of its patients.
> The hospital takes great care of its patients' security

There is no point in providing hooks if there is nothing to hang on them, so if you're going to work out where to put the apostrophe on the owner, you first have to know what is owned, once that is clear, circle the owner's name.

> The ⟮ticket machine⟯s power supply
> The ⟮security officer⟯s explanation
> A ⟮car⟯s turning circle

Step 9: Be clear and persuasive

The apostrophe is placed on the circle:
   The ticket machine's power supply
   The security officer's explanation
   A car's turning circle

In all the examples that follow, imagine drawing the circle. If the owner's name ends in 's' anyway, you can add apostrophe and 's', or just add the apostrophe. Generally, adding the apostrophe only is more common today.
   Charles' van
   Mrs James' explanation

If the owners' names are plural, they are likely to end in 's', so just add the apostrophe.
   Drivers' attitude
   Security officers' uniforms

If the plural doesn't end in 's', add the apostrophe and the 's'.
   Children's centre
   People's interest

The same rules apply for acronyms.
   The VIN's location
   GPs' attitude to private healthcare.

It's difficult to know what to do about its. Actually it's easier than it seems – the rule is: if 'its' is replacing 'it is', it needs an apostrophe; if it isn't, it doesn't! Note: this also applies to 'it has'.

Step 9: Be clear and persuasive

It's the first time we have ...
It's been a month since its opening.
Where are its instructions?
What is its sell-by date?
It's not working, its batteries are flat.

Test ten *insert the apostrophes where needed*

1 The Finance Directors question

2 The directors questions about the websites security

3 Carolines concerns about safety

4 Drivers unwillingness to park under the ash trees

5 The Estates Managers concern

6 Don't park in the GPs car park spaces

7 UNISONs advice on subsidised parking

8 Charles car is in the consultants car park

9 Changes to the bus routes have affected the number of staff driving to work

10 Mrs Smiths complaint about the ticket machines display

Answers are at the back of the book

Hyphens

Mother to be attacked in hospital car park (it's a plan!)
Mother-to-be attacked in hospital car park (an assault on a pregnant woman).

Step 9: Be clear and persuasive

It is difficult to give definite rules for the hyphen because it is so flexible, moving with the times and changing with the intended meaning. The simplest rule is to say that if two (or more) words need to be 'glued' together to have the meaning you intend, a hyphen is the glue.

> Following an in-depth survey, the board have concluded
> We should consider the range of products for not-for-profit organisations.
> It's a loss-making car park.

Where a word is in two parts and the join forms a commonly recognised letter pattern (e.g. ee, oo) it is better to use a hyphen than form them into one word.

> No-one (not noone)
> Co-operate (not cooperate)

Read it aloud, check and double-check it, ask a colleague to have a look. It's better they find a mistake than the committee does.

Step 10 — Write a good summary

There are two types of summary in business reports. The first, most important and most common is the one that appears at the front of the report. Usually called 'summary', it may also appear under the headings of 'executive summary', 'management summary', abstract or the more modern 'need to know'.

The second type of summary appears on templates where there is just a small box headed 'summary'. Either of these might be transferred to the minutes, but it is more likely that this second, smaller version will be used.

It is essential that the summary gives the key information and makes sense as a piece of writing on its own. It should be written on the basis that it will be all that the readers read ... a rather sobering thought for writers. The summary should be like a wool sweater accidentally put through on the hot wash: the same shape, colour and design, but much smaller and 'harder'.

The summary should be written last, although it will appear first. It should summarise the whole report from introduction through to recommendation.

Write a good summary

Most report writers find the summary incredibly difficult to write. If you have laboured through the writing of four pages, it is difficult to reduce it to a few paragraphs. There are two techniques which may help.

Return to the report skeleton

At the end of Step 5 you have a report skeleton – the headings and numbering in place, but no text. If you have to write a summary, save that as a separate document before continuing. Otherwise, just save the report as a new document, then delete the text, returning to the skeleton.

For each heading, think back and identify the key point(s) you wanted to get over the writer in that section, and type it under the heading. When you've done all of them, delete the headings and you will be left with the key points – these can now be re-written into the summary.

Identify key points

You may prefer to print a copy of your report and use a highlighter to mark the key points; again these will be re-written into the summary.

At the end of the book you'll find an example report – the car park 6 example that we've used throughout. Below are the summary and minutes summary:

Write a good summary

Example report (car park 6) – **a good summary**

Shortage of car park spaces is an ongoing problem at the hospital and in car park six there is the additional problem of old and unrealiable ticket machines. This causes problems for patients and visitors, and takes staff time in handling complaints.

As the lines in car park six need to be repainted, there is the opportunity to change the layout of the car park to a herringbone design. It is expected that this will reduce the number of minor accidents in the car park and give an extra eight spaces which will increase revenue.

Installation of pay-on-foot machines work will enable drivers to pay with a card, will increase revenue and save staff time

The cost of £64,800 should be recouped by the increased revenue in around 15 months.

Example report (car park 6) – **a brief minutes summary**

Changing the layout of the car park to a herringbone design should reduce the number of minor accidents and give an extra 24 spaces. A change to pay-on-foot parking will improve driver experience, increase revenue and save staff time. The cost of £64,800 should be recoupled in 15 months.

Write a good summary

Have a go

Identify the key point(s) made by the following three paragraphs.

1. The lines in the central car park were painted in 2009 when the staff car park was created, using a new paint with a rubber compound for durability. Seven years later they are still in excellent condition and need no repair.

2. The lines in car parks three, four and five, sited along the southern boundary of the site are showing signs of wear. They are generally still visible but in poor weather conditions are not so clear. This can result in cars being parked over the lines which wastes valuable space. Although not a priority for spending this year, work on these will be needed in 2018/19.

3. The lines in the car park six exit car park are almost completely worn away resulting in cars being badly parked which wastes space. A generally less kempt look seems to result in less respect for the environment and there is noticeably more litter in this car park that the others. The lines will be repainted over the coming summer.

Model answers are at the back of the book

Return to the summary after a while, does it make sense and send the right message if read alone?

Example report (persuade)

Example report (car park 6) *car park 6 — I want*

I want to redesign car park 6 and change to pay-on-foot parking

Example report (car park 6) *car park 6 — who's reading it*

Estates/facilities sub-committee

Example report (car park 6) *car park 6 — their perspective*

They probably don't know much, not really on their radar.

They'll be concerned to ensure costs covered by increased income, maybe press comment.

Example report (car park 6) *car park 6 — I need them to*

Allocate £64,800 for the redesign of car park six and the change to pay-on-foot parking.

Example report (persuade)

Improvements to Car Park 6

Report to the Finance Committee, March 2017

1. **Introduction**

    Shortage of car park spaces is an ongoing problem at the hospital which causes problems for patients and visitors, and takes staff time in handling complaints. The lines in car park 6, on the old community hospital site, are almost worn away which results in drivers leaving excess space between cars, leading to the equivalent of five spaces in each row left unused. As the lines need to be repainted, there is the opportunity to change the layout of the parking without the expenditure of a total removal of the old paint. The car park is currently 'pay-and-display' with old and increasingly unreliable ticket machines. Staff time is taken in checking tickets and emptying the machines, and attempts to tamper with the machines to steal the contents are increasing.

2. **Layout**

    2.1 **Problems with current layout**

    The current layout of car park 6 is the same as that in the other car parks with rows of spaces at a $90°$ angle. Drivers are able to drive forward or reverse into a space. There is a high number of minor scrapes which are expensive for drivers to repair and some try to blame the trust because of 'poor design'.

Example report (persuade)

The car park is made up of six rows of 24 spaces each with a ticket machine at each end. The corners at the end of each row are tight and lanes are of minimum width which can cause problem if two wider vehicles need to pass, particularly where a car is not parked well into the space. (See Appendix 1, Site Plan)

2.2 **The herringbone layout**

In a herringbone layout, the spaces are painted at 45° to the lanes and drivers enter them forwards. The lane is one-way only which can use the same entry and exit points as the current layout. (See Appendix 1, Site Plan)

(a) **Benefits of the herringbone layout**
The layout results in the same number of spaces in each row. However, one-way traffic and the reduction of space needed to enter/exit the spaces means that the lanes are narrower and this will mean a complete new row of spaces can be provided. This will take the total number of spaces to around 168. Patients and visitors will benefit from the extra spaces and the trust will benefit from the additional revenue.

(b) **Reduced number of accidents**
At present, there are frequent parking scrapes, either where drivers touch the neighbouring car as they enter/exit a space or when passing in the lanes. Although clearly not the trust's responsibility, some drivers seek to blame the car park layout and this takes up time and resources in dealing with the enquiries, looking for camera evidence, etc.

(c) **Works needed**

Three quotes have been obtained. Removing existing lines is expensive, so the cost of the work required is minimised by the fact that the lines are already badly worn. The remainder of the old lines will need to be removed and the new lines painted, using thermoplastic paint for longevity. The new lines will be painted in the herringbone layout with the necessary road arrows and lines.

3. Ticket machines

3.1 Existing payment arrangements

There are currently two pay-and-display machines; they are old and frequently break down which results in problems for visitors, loss of revenue and staff time taken in repairing them. There have been four recent attempts to break into the machines, one of which was successful. The security team patrols the car park daily to check for cars without tickets and penalty charge notices are issued; however this takes significant time in terms of the patrol and the administrative time in chasing payment.

3.2 Pay-on-foot car parking

The main hospital site operates a pay-on-foot system whereby visitors take a ticket at the entry barrier, pay for it on departure (either at main exit points or in the car park) and use the ticket to operate the exit barrier. Drivers are able to use debit/credit cards or cash. This system works well and has brought increased revenue as visitors cannot avoid paying, and pay for the actual time parked. It has also reduced the staffing costs of patrolling and administering the car park. The machines more secure and considerably quicker to operate than the existing machines.

(a) **Works needed**
Three quotes have been obtained. Entry and exit barriers will to be installed with the machines to dispense the ticket and operate the exit barrier. Payment machines will be sited at the entrance to the building and in the car park.

4. Investment and financial return

4.1 Investment

Removal of the remaining lines, repaint in herringbone format, paint in necessary arrows, traffic lines and disabled parking marks, install traffic signs	£2,450
Installation of entry and exit barriers with ticket machines	£26,500
Two payment machines	£36,850
Total	**£64,800**

4.2 Financial return

Additional annual income from 24 spaces (estimated)	**£51,900**

Example report (persuade)

On the basis of the figures above, the cost will have been repaid in 15 months
(Costings are attached as Appendix 2)

5. **Conclusion**

As the work to the car park is urgently needed, the change of design and ticketing will improve the patient/visitor experience and reduce staff costs, repaying the investment in just over a year.

6. **Recommendation**

That the board allocates £64,800 for:
- the change of design of car park 6
- the change to pay-on-foot parking

Appendices

1. Plan of car park 6 showing existing layout and herringbone layout.

2. Detail of costings.

Example report (inform)

Example report (annual review) *annual report — notice?*

It's all OK

Example report (annual review) *annual report — who's reading it*

Finance committee

Example report (annual review) *annual report — their perspective*

They are well-informed and familiar but it's the first time it has been a stand-alone report.

It's in their remit but one of things that just 'ticks over', vaguely interested but not particularly bothered

Example report (inform)

Car Parking at Henrow City Hospital

Report to Estates and Facilities Sub-committee

21 June 2017

1. **Introduction**

    Changes in the board reporting system have resulted in the requirement for a separate annual report on car parking to the estates and facilities sub-committee. This report gives an overview of parking and an update for 2016/17.

2. **Background**

    When the hospital opened in 1958, there were two small car parks offering 150 spaces. With additions to the hospital, the car park also grew and in 1998 there were around 1,350 spaces. The purchase of the community hospital site in 2008 brought a further 200 spaces, and changes to the design and layout of the car parks now means there is a total of 1,580 spaces available, 400 of which are for staff use.

3. **Car park provision**

    At the start of 2016, the car parks were renamed to link to the colour zones used throughout the hospital. This was reinforced by painting the top bar of the fences and by colour co-ordinated signs. This has proved popular with users.

Example report (inform)

Car park	Spaces
Orange	340
Yellow	326
Green	210
Purple	160
Car park 6	144

There is a total of 1,180 spaces of which around 56% are sited near the main ward block, 30% are nearer the outpatients and clinic sites and the remainder are on the old community hospital site.

The car on the old community hospital site is still known as car park 6, but this will be changed to the blue car park when the work on its design and payment arrangements is complete.

There is a significant shortage of car parking which causes complaints from patients and visitors, and causes problems with patients arriving late to clinics and staff to meetings.

4. Finance

4.1 Charges

Charging was simplified in April 2016 and is currently:

20 minutes	free
1 hour	£2.00
2 hours	£3.00
3 hours	£4.00
6 hours	£6.00
24 hours	£8.00

Offering 20 minutes free is popular with people who only wish to deliver to the hospital and means that if the car park is full, drivers can exit to try another without incurring a charge.

Example report (inform)

Free parking is offered to patients with regular, lengthy appoints (e.g. dialysis, chemotherapy) and to visitors for intensive care. There are also disabled parking spaces in each car park and users can get their ticket validated to remove the charge at the information desk. Few people take up this option.

4.2 **Revenue**

Revenue from the car parks in 2016/17 totalled £1,230, a slight increase on last year.

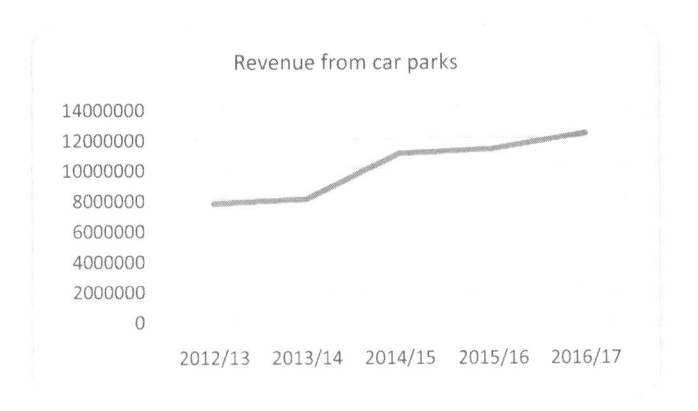

Revenue from car parks

| | 2012/13 | 2013/14 | 2014/15 | 2015/16 | 2016/17 |

The rise in revenue in 2014/5, resulted from the change from pay-and-display to pay-on-foot parking in the four main car parks. It is expected there will be a small rise next year when car park 6 is changed to pay-on-foot parking.

The revenue funds the repair and maintenance of the car parks, security and the park-and-ride system.

5. User satisfaction

Views on car parking were specifically sought in the 2016 satisfaction survey. Generally, the quality of the car parks and cleanliness attracted compliments, as did dealings with staff on parking issues.

Difficulty in parking was the main cause for complaints, followed by charging, although the survey was carried out just after national press covering on hospital charges for parking. It is the difficulty in parking which is the cause of most formal complaints received by the department.

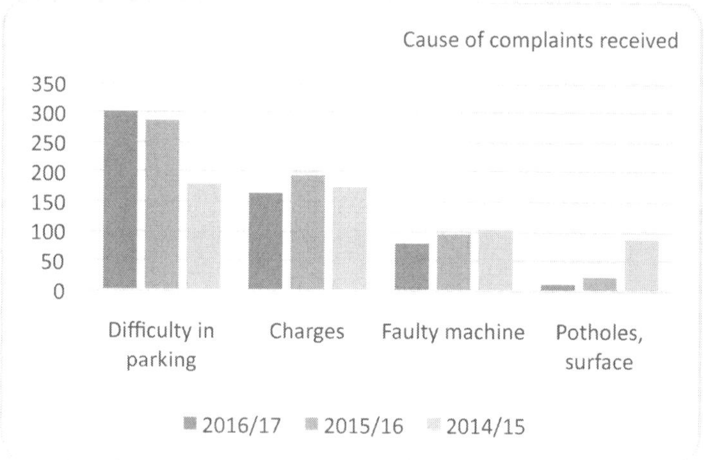
Cause of complaints received
350
300
250
200
150
100
50
0
Difficulty in parking
Charges
Faulty machine
Potholes, surface
2016/17
2015/16
2014/15

The park-and-ride system has eased the problem, but talks with the local bus company have not been successful, as there would not be the financial return to justify routing the buses to the hospital. It is expected that difficulty in parking will continue to be as issue because there are not enough spaces for the visitor numbers at the site.

6. Health & safety

The only reported incidents have been classed as minor, for example, overhanging branches or unclear signage, and these have been dealt with as they arose.

Car park 6 has been the cause of several traffic incidents – scrapes and bumps due to the narrow lane width. Although not serious, they are expensive for those involved and some people have attempted to blame the trust because of the poor design of the car park. It is expected that this will cease to be a problem when the new layout is in place.

6.1 Risk assessment

The annual risk assessment has been completed with no significant risks identified.

7. Recommendation

That the Estates and Facilities Sub-committee notes the report.

Answers

Plain English

1. The pay and display machine has broken down five times in the last three months.

2. The June 2016 report ...

3. Shortage of car park spaces is an ongoing problem at the hospital which causes problems for patients and visitors, and takes staff time in handling complaints.

    The lines in car park 6, on the old community hospital site, are almost worn away, which results in drivers leaving excess space between cars, leading to the equivalent of five spaces in each row left unused. As the lines need to be repainted, there is the opportunity to change the layout of the parking without the expenditure of a total removal of the old paint.

    The car park is currently 'pay-and-display', with old and increasingly unreliable ticket machines. Staff time is taken in checking tickets and emptying the machines, and attempts to tamper with the machines to steal the contents are increasing.

4. Three quotes have been obtained. Removing existing lines is expensive, so the work required and, therefore, cost is minimised by the fact that the lines are already badly worn. The remainder of the old lines will need to be removed and the new lines painted, using thermoplastic paint for

Answers

longevity. The new lines will be painted in the herringbone layout with the necessary road arrows and lines.

5   Drivers are used to pay-on-foot, as it is commonly used in public car parks.

6   The charges must be seen as fair, or drivers will ty to avoid payment.

7   The parking attendant's reaction ...

8   The security staff accept that the current overtime arrangements are likely to change and they expect the union's support if they are asked to work only their contracted hours.

9   The board believes that the hospital's parking problems are the result of the cancellation of the 2015 contract with PayCo Machine Services.

10 Each stage in the project is marked as 'red' when overdue, 'amber' when in-hand and 'green' when completed.

11 An in-depth analysis of the figures has shown ...

12 The arrows can be painted once the lines have been completed.

13 Payment can be made with the new £1 coin.

14 Disabled drivers can park free-of-charge.
    (or)
    Parking is free for disabled drivers.

15 There will be a plan to deal with problems whilst the car park is closed.

16 The priority is the safety of drivers.

17 The condition of the tarmac is adequate.

Answers

Punctuation

Comma, semi-colon and colon

1. People who use the 'help' button on the payment machines are directed to the security office, however this is often not staffed.

2. The lines in the central staff car park are clearly visible; those in car parks 4, 5 and 6 are worn but visible and don't need attention this year; most lines in the West End exit car park urgently need repainting.

3. According to the Director of Estates and Facilities, "Car parks have been identified as a priority for 2018/19."

4. Eventually he admitted why he hadn't reported the damage to his vehicle: he had caused it himself reversing into a bollard.

5. Eventually he admitted why he hadn't reported the damage to his vehicle; the accident form was completed and the file closed.

6. Numberplate recognition cameras will be installed in:
    - central car park
    - car park 4
    - car park 6.

7. Numberplate recognition cameras will be installed in central car park, car park 4 and car park 6.

8. Numberplate recognition cameras sites: central car park, car park 4 and car park 6.

9. I enclose your 2017/18 parking permit; please stick this on your windscreen, ideally in the top left corner.

10. There are 900 spaces in car park 4, six of which are for disabled users, and a further 600 in car park 5.

Answers

Apostrophe

1. The Finance Director's question
2. The directors' questions about the website's security
3. Caroline's concerns about safety
4. Drivers' unwillingness to park under the ash trees
5. The Estates Manager's concern
6. Don't park in the GPs' car park spaces
7. UNISON's advice on subsidised parking
8. Charles' car is in the consultants' car park
9. Changes to the bus routes have affected the number of staff driving to work
10. Mrs Smith's complaint about the ticket machine's display

Writing a summary

1. The lines in central car park are in excellent condition.

2. The lines in car parks 3, 4 and 5 are showing signs of wear and will need repainting in 2018/19

3. The lines in car park six are completely worn and will be repainted in the coming summer.

These would be run together to read:

The lines in central car park are in excellent condition; those in car parks 3, 4 and 5 are showing signs of wear and will need repainting in 2018/19; in car park 6 the lines are completely worn and will be repainted in the coming summer.